To Pc
Pa

the difference between failure & Success often lies between our own Two ears.

Best Wishes

Path to Success

Ray Matthews

The Book Guild Ltd

First published in Great Britain in 2023 by
The Book Guild Ltd
Unit E2 Airfield Business Park,
Harrison Road, Market Harborough,
Leicestershire. LE16 7UL
Tel: 0116 2792299
www.bookguild.co.uk
Email: info@bookguild.co.uk
Twitter: @bookguild

Copyright © 2023 Ray Matthews

The right of Ray Matthews to be identified as the author of this
work has been asserted by them in accordance with the
Copyright, Design and Patents Act 1988.

All rights reserved. No part of this publication may be
reproduced, transmitted, or stored in a retrieval system, in any form or by any means,
without permission in writing from the publisher, nor be otherwise circulated in
any form of binding or cover other than that in which it is published and without
a similar condition being imposed on the subsequent purchaser.

Typeset in 12pt Minion Pro

Printed and bound by CPI Group (UK) Ltd, Croydon, CR0 4YY

ISBN 978 1915603 524

British Library Cataloguing in Publication Data.
A catalogue record for this book is available from the British Library.

This book is dedicated to my wife and soulmate Maureen in appreciation of her unselfish continued support over the past sixty-odd years. Without her encouragement and just being there my challenges would never have been possible. Thank you.

Contents

Prologue ix

1. I Wanna Be A Boxer 1
2. My Seventy-Five-Marathon Challenge 16
3. From the Red Lion to Phoenix 39
4. Nipples of steel 59
5. From school to Steelos 84
6. Don't look, Maureen 104
7. KO for anti-boxing campaigners 128
8. Following in Ivanhoe's footsteps 146
9. Introduction to boxing's dark side 169
10. Two marathons, one civic reception 189
11. Sammy returns to haunt me 208
12. Don't mess with a little old lady from Dalton 233
13. Fulfilling my promise to Newman School 256
14. London calling 268

Epilogue 285
Acknowledgements 289

Prologue

The great thing about writing your very own biography, I reckon, is that as time passes there are no rules or script to follow. Just memories of life as it were, life as it unfolded, and hopes for the future.

In an effort to provide the best reading experience from this, my latest book, I believe have successfully managed to highlight some of the most memorable and interesting moments in my life.

There are many friends to thank along the way, particularly over the past decade during the many crazy challenges I have set myself. I have provided them with the opportunity to recount their stories, memories and experiences alongside mine.

Now here's the twist. Rather than place these stories at the beginning or tuck them away at the end of the book, you will find them strategically placed at the end of relevant chapters adding, perhaps, a different perspective as the story unfolds.

These people have varying backgrounds and different roles in my story. One thing that they have in common is that they are all valued, trusted friends.

And for that very special friend who asked to be featured in my book. No worries, mate, you're in, but you're brutally bumped off on page 75!

1
I Wanna Be A Boxer

'*Could do better...*'

Hands up how many of you received that statement on the bottom of your year-end school report in the comments column? Well, I am embarrassed to say I did, year on year.

Often, when I think back to my school days, now over seventy years ago, this comment – attached alongside all the academic subjects – comes flooding back and is probably one of the most stand-out influential memories of my Roman Catholic education.

The eldest of four brothers, it was down to me to set the standards, forging the way for my siblings to follow. That's what big brothers do, after all, isn't it?

As I recall, when that perennial envelope was opened at home, my dad would shake his head and say to Mum in disgust, 'I told you so,' as he read through the low marked results and offered the same comments every year. My academic education was a great deal substandard to the one he had received all those years previous at South Grove School.

Even though this annual routine created a heated debate between them, there was never any real suggestion made to change schools.

At St Bede's Roman Catholic School in Masbrough, Rotherham, we weren't taught what my dad always advocated should have been compulsory in all schools: subjects like woodwork, metalwork and science that needed laboratory equipment. Art, albeit in a very restricted form, came into the curriculum during my latter two years.

We were briefly taught Latin, much used in the day-to-day Catholic teachings and, of course, predominantly used during Mass. Latin always seemed a complete waste of time to me, although, strangely enough, much of what I was taught I can still remember. During a caning session in the headmaster's office for fighting (again), one particular phrase, "Sui generis", was addressed at me with venom, together with a suggestion that I should investigate the meaning as a form of penance.

I had received this comment from our smarty-pants headmaster, who obviously had a master's degree in the subject.

We even had to march – usually single file on a Monday morning with our Woolworths pumps hanging round our necks – down to a private gymnasium opposite where Rotherham United's magnificent New York football stadium has since been built.

Everything else to do with games and sport took place on the school's split-level sloping tarmac playground, with goal posts and cricket stumps painted on the outside toilet wall.

Our yearly tuition was administered in the same drab

classroom by one teacher who taught every academic subject that formed our day-to-day education.

On reflection, I was never likely to have had the opportunity to become academically educated enough to take a place at Oxford or Cambridge.

It was because of Mum's influence that her four boys would be brought up as Catholic and I suppose my dad must have agreed at some time, although he never stopped comparing his own education to the lack of mine.

Even though I did pass my eleven-plus exam, I readily accepted the fact that higher education was never on the cards for me, mainly because of the additional costs attached to my continued higher education.

We could never in a million years afford for me to go to the Christian Brothers at De La Salle College in Sheffield, the Catholic equivalent of a grammar school education. The cost of bus fares from Rotherham to Sheffield, books, pens and pencils, not to mention the mandatory college uniform, all made for an impossible step forward for me. Only the wealthiest of my mates made the transition from St Bede's to a much higher education.

I really didn't care about the academic side of school studies after that, which became the turning point in my education. So, the decision during the early years of my life was to continue at St Bede's, with my new aim of managing to get through by doing the bare minimum.

When I look back on those early years, my overall recollection is that as a family we were always on the edge of destitution; struggling to make ends meet was an under-statement.

My father, suffering at that time with a slipped disc, was hospitalised for months on end and eventually brought home by ambulance, cocooned in a plaster cast jacket from neck to lower waist and unable to work for around seven years.

We survived by the skin of our teeth, mainly because of my mum's ability to provide just enough for us to get through. Mum was a talented singer who sang under the stage name 'Marion Taylor' at the many working men's clubs around Rotherham and surrounding areas, booked to perform most weekends and the odd midweek session.

The local music halls and affiliated working men's clubs, where Mum regularly sang, provided much-needed evening entertainment during a time of re-building after the war and were a major part of northern communities back then.

Families benefited from trips and seaside days away, with busloads of excited children boarding rickety old buses in anticipation of a day at the beach. One of the committee members would hand out an envelope containing two florins (that's twenty pence to you young 'uns) spending money to each child as they noisily boarded. Cleethorpes, Bridlington and Skegness were regular coastal destinations.

I would often accompany my mum around the clubs, carrying her music score in an old brown leather suitcase, bussing it everywhere around Rotherham, Sheffield and Doncaster. She had a varied repertoire including ballads and the popular songs of the time. It all depended on audience participation; Mum had a knack of knowing which songs would go down well. She had also mastered a couple of classical arias which, if the pianist had the ability to play and accompany her, of course, would dramatically wrap up her night's performance with clasped hands on one knee.

My first taste of showbiz life, I suppose. I thoroughly enjoyed mixing with the friendly entertainers, many of whom were cutting their teeth in the working men's clubs on their way to ultimate TV stardom.

I particularly enjoyed watching comedians and, towards the end of Mum's singing career in the late fifties, my parents took me to see a show at Brown Street Working Men's Club not far from our house in Masbrough. On the bill was Charlie Adolphus Williams. If you've never heard of him, just Google Charlie Williams. He was an ex-professional footballer, singer and Britain's first black stand-up comedian. His humour may not have been to everyone's taste, but it had me in stitches.

I had been used to being banned from sitting out in the audience areas of the clubs. 'Not for your ears, young man,' the adults would say if the comedians were a bit raunchy, or worse. That didn't stop me listening anyway from behind the stage curtains. I always had a good joke to tell my mates in those days.

Mum was a very popular club artist, her diary constantly full; she was always rebooked by the club secretary before leaving to catch the last bus, often not getting home much before midnight.

Certainly, without the income provided by Mum's singing, times would have been even worse. There were no government handouts back then for destitute families. Before the advent of the NHS in 1948, there was no such thing as free health care, which was always in big demand for a young family of four boys growing up in the forties. Everything we now take for granted didn't exist back then, during and after the war. The prospect of our family ending up in the workhouse was a stark reality. Seriously.

It was a tough old life in those early days but just normal for me – nobody had owt to brag about anyway. We never went hungry, though. Mum always made sure there was plenty of good, wholesome food on the table. First up was usually best dressed as my brothers, Alan, Peter and David, became much more the same size.

As a young boy growing up in the forties, the responsibility for looking after my younger brothers was a heavy burden to accept. At times I would rebel and disappear on my own for the day just to escape. Having said all that, I was allowed the freedom that enabled me to live a life that today's kids will never experience. We instinctively knew who the dodgy characters around town were and we avoided them like the plague with a TomTom-like warning system that worked well between friends.

At a very early age, I became streetwise and well educated in life skills. I became a dab hand at avoiding the milkman, coal man, rent man and anyone else who came knocking on our back door looking for money. When answering the door as the front man, so to speak, I became fluent with excuses as they came for their weekly dues and demands. It was like playing a game of who would get paid that week, which became part of our normal day-to-day existence.

My education from the 'school of life' provided the knowledge I would need in readiness for the big bad world. Who could want for more?

Anyway, my future was always going to be great and, with the confidence that only a fourteen-year-old could possess, I was ready and eager for the next phase of my life.

My future was already mapped out as I approached the last year at St Bede's, because I'd decided I was going to be either a professional footballer or boxer.

Decision-making time became necessary during a meeting

with my new coach, Jacky Pearson, at the Steel, Peech and Tozer boxing gym, aka Phoenix Boxing Club, on Sheffield Road.

'You are going to have to make your mind up which you want to do well at. Football and boxing don't mix without a compromise on performance. It's either one or the other.'

That comment from Jacky came just before my fifteenth birthday and took me by surprise. Now, looking back, I can appreciate his concern as I had suffered a leg injury during a midweek school's football cup semi-final that had put the kybosh on my boxing training for over a couple of weeks.

Only that week had I spent some time in talks about my future with my teacher, Mr Flynn. High on the agenda was my prospects based around a future in the football profession after leaving school.

Schooling during my last two years at St Bede's had been under the fairest but hardest of taskmasters, Mr Flynn. He, more than any of the other teachers, had the greatest influence on my life. We discussed his concerns about my footballing prospects and the ramifications of putting all my eggs in one basket at such a young age.

Mr Flynn, who possessed English FA coaching qualifications, had spent hours with me during and occasionally out of school hours, coaching and steering me during two very successful years. Our school team had won far more matches in the Rotherham Schools' football league than had ever been achieved by a St Bede's team in the past.

As school captain for sport at that time, I loved football and, now playing for Rotherham Juniors, had exciting dreams for the future.

'Ray, no matter how talented you are as a junior footballer, it does not always mature into senior talent.'

Disappointing, but true and wise words that I remember well today. Realism.

Taking that knock-back on the chin, the decision I was about to make with Jacky Pearson became a relatively easy one. I would follow my first love and devote all my time and energies into boxing with the hope of one day turning professional.

'I am going to do better.'

I have made necessary decisions at every crossroads in my life – impulsive and life-changing at times – but right or wrong they had to be made at that time and often, even though available, without parental guidance.

Of course, I will never know what the outcome would have been if I had taken a different path and I suppose it's true to say you can't change the past anyway. But I can recall what I have been through and where the different journeys have led me up until now. On reflection, it's not been a bad old life to date.

The rest of my life, however short it may be, has yet to be determined by the choices I will continue to make as I work my way up to and beyond my eightieth year.

*

Right then, who's up for coming along on my eventful journey to date? You know you want to!

OK then, let's bring you up to date and get rolling into a life full of ups, a few downs and then even more ups.

We'll make a start with that very first life-changing

decision I had to make as a ten-year-old ginger-haired, short-trousered rebel who was always in trouble.

When I decided I needed to learn how to box, little did I realise that I was about to meet a man who would change my life forever.

Sometime shortly before my tenth birthday, the rest of my life got underway when, for the very first time, I set foot into the smoke-filled tap room of the Red Lion pub in Rotherham town centre. The landlord pulling pints behind the bar pointed an outstretched arm to a dark green door in the corner. A door that I opened, with trepidation running through my body, a door which led me up the thirteen dimly lit creaking steps to the Red Lion Boxing Club above the packed, noisy pub.

My heart pumping like mad and legs nearly buckling under me, I stopped halfway and thought about turning back and going home while I still had the chance. But somehow I managed to reach the door above, confronting the immense fear I felt in the pit of my stomach.

Knocking on that dark green door was one of the hardest decisions I have ever made in my life; waiting for a response seemed like an eternity.

On the second knock the door eventually opened to reveal the silhouette of Benny Kemp, with shoulders the size of a barn door, a bent nose and cauliflower ears. But what really greeted me was all the action, atmosphere and noise from inside the room.

'What can we do for thee, young man?' he asked in a deep Yorkshire voice.

'I wanna be a boxer,' I remember saying with as much authority as I could muster.

'Reyt then,' he said with a smile on his face. 'Tha'd better come wi' me.' With hands the size of a frying pan firmly gripping my shoulders, he marched me inside the room.

The large, well-lit room was filled with around eight or nine professional (or so I presumed) boxers all going about their training: skipping, shadow boxing and punching the bags down the outside wall, with one extra-impressive big guy knocking hell out of a large bag in the corner of the room.

The centre of the room was dominated by the large three-roped boxing ring to which I was being fairly forcibly steered.

'Let's see what tha' made on then, young 'un,' Benny said, inviting me to climb into the ring.

What could be so difficult about getting into a ring, you may ask?

Now then, here's where I want you to use your imagination.

At ten years old, with legs shorter than average, it can be exceedingly difficult! Obviously, I made the wrong choice by attempting to get through between the top and middle ropes. Even on tiptoe, neither foot touched the floor, leaving me stranded in mid-air and in some pain from the nether regions and suspecting I would end up with a high-pitched soprano voice for some time to come!

But before I had time to evaluate the pain, I was being gloved up with a pair of ten-ounce dark brown leather gloves that were much older than me by the look of the wear and tear, especially the inside where the horsehair padding was escaping.

Another young boy, whom I had seen skipping close to the ring, was being gloved up and getting ready to step into the ring as my first-ever sparring partner.

Trying to describe the panic I was now experiencing

would only be grossly understated. This wasn't going at all as I expected it would.

I had anticipated that there would be a much gentler introduction. I'd naively presumed I would be shown around the gym and apparatus, perhaps invited to sit and watch with an explanation of what would be expected of me, etcetera. But no. Here I was in the ring facing an opponent who seemed to have grown a foot since entering the ring. He stood facing me with a look that said he was more than capable and about to take my head off my shoulders – and they didn't even know my name yet. Talk about being thrown into the lion's den…

'This lad will feyt thi,' Benny said. 'So let's see how tha' gets on wi' him.'

This arena in which I was now standing, with shaking legs and panicking almost out of control, was taking up around twenty-four square feet in the centre of the room. The ring, getting smaller by the second, was made up with three red-brown two-inch diameter fraying hemp ropes with what appeared to be padded pillowcases hung over each corner to cover the steel rope adjusters. The dark grey canvas floor, splattered in archaic dried blood stains, was pegged down and extended a good foot beyond the outside of the ropes.

Could Benny see the panic in my eyes, I remember wondering, as the adrenaline of fear that was running through my body turned into the adrenaline of despair in one fell swoop. I don't think it would have made any difference at all.

How would I best go about showing what I was capable of against this experienced-looking giant in the ring?

I didn't have much time to dwell as Benny shouted time and my opponent swiftly advanced towards me throwing punches, with one or two connecting, almost before I had moved. Hell's bells! There was no sparring around or niceties for the new boy, leaving me with no other option but to get stuck in as survival mode kicked in.

I don't remember much more after that but, in what seemed like no time at all, I was being dragged off him to shouts of, 'Stop! Stop!' from Benny.

As I came to from this dissociative experience, I suddenly realised that my opponent was cowering in the corner with me raining punches on him. I was out of breath but felt slightly upset at being forcibly stopped.

'Reyt, we now know tha' can feyt,' said Benny as he steered me over to the corner of the ring to where I had first had the gloves fitted. 'Now let's see how tha' gets on wi' a boxer,' indicating to a lanky lad called "Cloggy Clarke", I later found out, to get gloved up.

Benny spent a couple of minutes providing instructions on how best to deal with a boxer, whilst my next sparring partner was having his gloves laced up, none of which entered my brain.

Oh hell. As I turned to face my next sparring partner, I quickly realised this one looked like he really did know how to box. He slipped gracefully into the ring, facing me square-on and stood, intimidatingly ready to perform. I was fearing the worst, long before Benny shouted time for the second time. Cloggy, looking every bit the part of a professional boxer, worked his way towards me with arms held high, providing me with no target at all.

He was a good two inches taller than me, but skinny. As he advanced towards me, I was stood rooted to the spot in fear. It soon became evident that he possessed far more arms than me; punches rained down from every direction possible and at a speed with which I couldn't cope, making it a one-way fight that was definitely not in my favour.

I couldn't get near him! The boxing skills he clearly possessed were always going to make a scrapper like me come off second best and some of the punches he caught me with blinking well hurt! Covering up became number-one priority, trying to avoid a real good hiding, while frustratingly not knowing how to deal with his skills. I should have listened more intently to Benny!

I did catch Cloggy with a cracking right-hander that slowed him down a bit and probably made him aware that I could strike back – if he let me get near him, of course.

His footwork was flawless, matching his ability to punch me at speed and move out of the way fast enough to keep me from getting within striking distance. I was breathing out of my backside after only a minute or so and struggled to keep going, throwing punch after punch in a windmill-like attempt as I chased him round the ring in temper trying to land another punch.

Time was called. I was in a trance-like state but couldn't feel any blood running from me anywhere. I had survived my first real boxing lesson.

Benny walked over to me as I stood in shock. He led me back to the corner and untied my gloves, asking me to stuff the horsehair padding back into place. One round was more than enough for me to realise that I had a hell of a lot to learn if I wanted to become a boxer.

'Well done, young 'un, I think we can make summat of thi' if tha' still wants to be a boxer. What's thi' name, lad? Tha gonna need a skipping rope, pumps, shorts and vest. Training is Tuesday and Thursday evenings, 6:30 till 8:30, and Saturday mornings 10 till 12. The subs are tuppence a week.'

Flipping 'eck. I'd never even considered that I would have to pay owt. I'd have to tell Mum and Dad what I was up to now. Before that, I hadn't told a soul of my intentions, not even my brothers.

I ran all the way home from the Red Lion Yard, just off All Saints' Square.

'I'm gonna be a boxer,' I kept telling myself, gliding home up Brown Street and on to Holland Place on adrenaline.

And a world-champion boxer at that!

Unbeknown to me at the time, Benny Kemp was destined to make a huge difference, changing my whole way of life forever and packing such a powerful punch, pardon the pun.

And just between us, but don't say owt, I never had to pay subs – ever!

As I put pen to paper today (so to speak) and wipe away the sweat off my brow in recollection of the fear and sustained effort of that first encounter in the ring, I feel a sense of pride that I survived that very first episode and had the guts to say yes. Because what quickly followed was an exciting progression on my way to a fair few successful years of boxing.

My desire to learn how to box in the first place was to exact retribution on the bullies who had plagued my life because of my ginger hair. There is a certain irony as those bullies, unknowingly, were the catalyst for one of the major turning points in my young life.

I was about to head off in a direction of new disciplines and learning that would have the greatest influence on the rest of my life. But best of all, after word got out about my boxing, I never had to fight at school again.

Right from the outset, one of the first disciplines that was drummed into me was the code of conduct. I was learning how to inflict pain and use boxing as a form of self-defence to look after myself, but I was taught that I must never take advantage of these new skills by using them outside of the ring. Boxing also gave me the means and discipline to control my fiery temper – a new Ray.

2

My Seventy-Five-Marathon Challenge

The difference between failure and success often lies between our own two ears. It's also worth mentioning that, in my experience, many people are afraid to succeed due to the overbearing fear of failure and what other people may think. But, inevitably, failure and success are the two sides of the coin of life – your mindset influences and determines the outcome.

From an athletic viewpoint and your ability to fully analyse and understand that comment, you're either capable of running long distances or have contemplated having a go.

Let me offer a bit of advice, my friend, if you're new to this long-distance running malarkey. The ability to run long distances stems generally from having a mental strength that provides enough of an attitude and discipline to overrule the body's unwillingness to destroy itself. That's why, I presume, most runners won't ever run more than a marathon distance, because once you've tried you know it bloody well hurts.

Running (or walking) 26.2 miles requires many hours of enthusiasm, passion and disciplined training to achieve.

So, when you've put in the hard training sessions and the day finally arrives, you stand on the starting line of your first marathon. You will most likely have your target time in mind, but alongside you are other runners, who all look like seasoned athletes, and as the nerves kick in you start wondering what on earth you're doing there.

The gun goes off and away you go. The adrenaline fires up and you're soon being pulled along at a faster pace than you've trained for, keeping pace with your fellow runners. At first it feels comfortable and perhaps you're convinced you can run a faster time than predicted, thinking that you can coast in towards the end having gained an extra ten minutes or so. Then the lactic hits your legs and it seems like you've been running forever and you're wondering how many more miles to go.

Eventually the end is in sight, but not before you've been passed by a giraffe, a couple of rhinos and half a dozen Wombles. The euphoria of crossing that finish line finally comes as you stop your watch, determined that no additional time will be added to that small flashing screen on your wrist. You're dead and your legs come to a grinding halt, but against all your body's demands you can't stop. You're being encouraged to keep moving, otherwise you're going to get trampled to death by your fellow runners as they sprint through the finish line like a herd of stampeding cattle determined to get that personal best.

Body aching, heart pounding and lungs gasping for air, the coveted medal is placed around your neck from an overly cheerful lady who tells you, 'Well done, you're looking good,' when you feel like you're dying.

Two minutes later you're vowing never to run that distance ever again because the lactic acid has taken over; your legs have a mind of their own and it's impossible to walk without looking as though you've messed your pants. Oh, the pain, but the medal around your neck, which you've just admired for the tenth time and vowed that you're even going to bed with it on, makes it all worthwhile.

Finally, somehow you're back home, the stairs are a complete no-no and you're wishing you lived in a bungalow. It's much easier to walk backwards for a week. OK, so maybe I am exaggerating a bit. Or possibly not? You tell me!

Every athlete, from club runner to Olympian, will have a limit: their lactate threshold that forces them to stop. But, for some reason, not me. My body seems to defy what's normal and I am one of the lucky ones for whom lactic acid is not the big enemy. Well, that's my opinion and I'm open to comments, but I suppose that's partly the reason why I have been able to run long distances – such as the hundred- and 150-mile self-inflicted challenges in the recent past – without too much damage to muscles or tendons. Even racing across deserts has been pretty enjoyable. Honest!

*

Having the good fortune to be able to recover quickly after a long run has been a massive bonus, allowing me to train for these ultra-distances, often clocking up to 120 miles a week of training in readiness for these endurance challenges.

A few months after my seventy-first birthday, nine years ago, I managed to complete three consecutive circuits of the Rowbotham's Round Rotherham fifty-mile international trail race. By adding fifty miles either side of the main race, I completed the 150-mile challenge in a credible thirty-four hours. It was during this challenge that my latest so-called "hair-brained" challenge was hatched.

Running 150 miles in one go should have taken me to the edge of my capability. I should have been crawling across the finish line. I should have been completely spent and felt that I had finally reached that ultimate goal – that lactate threshold – or at least failed in the attempt. But at around the 130-mile mark, feeling far better than I could ever have dreamed I would be feeling and with just around twenty miles to go, I knew that this challenge was not going to have the desired end result I had anticipated.

The final stretch felt like I was running on auto-pilot, with my body allowing my brain to focus on what's next. This relentless distance was clearly not going to flatten me, so what challenge could possibly satisfy my ambition?

Over the next few miles, my mind in overdrive throwing various thoughts in the air simultaneously like a juggler with a handful of balls, the answer finally became obvious, causing me to laugh out loud.

The next milestone in my life was to be a significant one at that –well, certainly one that warranted some thoughts about what to do and ways of celebration. I would be seventy-five in a few years' time, so why not run seventy-five marathons in seventy-five days and start on my seventy-fifth birthday as a present to me?

Why ever not? It sounded good to me, and I was more than convinced that it was doable.

Going back to my opening comments, I would like to further add just a short observation.

Those who succeed will most likely have said, it may be difficult but it is possible; whereas those who say it may be possible but it will be difficult will probably fail.

Never fear failure; just being on the start line you're already a winner.

This would likely be the ultimate challenge I was looking for and served the two relevant purposes.

That was it. It was now set in stone. I was going to run seventy-five marathons in seventy-five days starting on my seventy-fifth birthday.

How could I have known, as I kicked that decision round and around in my head for a few weeks before finally making the announcement, that this challenge would completely turn my life upside-down and in directions that I would never have thought possible?

I have always advocated that the best way to keep the day-to-day passion alive and momentum moving forward is to always have the next challenge set up, or in mind, before the completion of the one you're doing. That way there is always something good to look forward to, keeping you from becoming bored and static.

Time marches on as it inevitably does and, after a couple of years or so in tick-over mode, thoughts returned to this self-inflicted challenge I had promised myself, a challenge I was determined to take on.

Having successfully completed the 150-mile challenge a couple of years previously, I was generally satisfied, other than the niggling disappointment at crossing the finish line at Dearne Valley College in Manvers half a minute after my predicted time of 10am.

It was now time to make a start on the huge amount of

planning that would inevitably be needed to take on the seventy-five marathons.

'Training can start in a few months. Plenty of time,' I thought.

During the next few months, the logistics of organising seventy-five marathons was becoming mentally challenging, a complete nightmare, to be honest, and I quickly realised that, without a huge amount of help, it would never get off the ground.

I needed help, big-style.

'This has got to be a world record,' I was being told by many after I had made public my intentions. This was one of the more constructive comments among many which indicated that I was completely mental and would surely die in the attempt.

If that was to be the case, I thought I probably ought to elevate this challenge even further.

How I was going to do that was a no-brainer. I wasn't just going to do this challenge for my own personal achievement; the drive, motivation and enormity would be used to benefit and inspire others less fortunate than most.

Newman School, situated in its own grounds on the outskirts of Rotherham, is such an amazing school which caters for children with a large variety of special educational needs, illnesses and disabilities. These children are looked after and educated by a team of highly dedicated angels. They were who I was going to run the seventy-five marathons for.

This wasn't to be the first time I had supported the school. I had managed to raise enough money after the 150-mile challenge to purchase a specially adapted trike for the school that would allow some of the children to ride a bike for the very first time.

I will never forget the joy and laughter from young Josh

as he rode the new trike for the first time, zooming down the corridor before turning into the main hall to meet the press and photographers. When it was time to let one of the other youngsters have a go he kept shaking his head and wouldn't get off.

'No, Ray's bought me this,' he kept saying.

That eventful official handover at Newman School ranks high on my great memory list. I was well and truly hooked, making myself a promise that very afternoon that whenever I had the opportunity to raise money during any future challenges, Newman School would take priority.

Shortly after deciding what my big birthday challenge would be, I visited the school and asked to see the headteacher, Julie Mott.

'Julie, I am about to take on a challenge that should allow me to raise a substantial amount of money for the school. What's top of your wish list? What would you like for the kids?' I asked her during the first of our marathon meetings.

She told me there were many things the children would greatly benefit from, but they were very expensive.

'Don't worry about the cost, just let me know what you want,' I told her.

We talked about the many items of equipment that would improve the children's experience at school, including swings and roundabouts that were accessible for wheelchair users. High on the wish list was the soft rubberising of the playgrounds to enable the children to play in safety.

I asked Julie to get a quote for everything we'd talked about and promised to meet back at school in a couple of weeks to establish just how much I needed to raise.

After signing out at reception, I walked out of school towards my car which was parked on the road outside the school. Before reaching the automatic gates I stopped and looked across to my right through the dark green open mesh fencing. The dense wooded area at the bottom of the school grounds glared back at me with a flood of ideas instantly zooming round in my head. The adrenaline caused by the excitement of my thoughts became equal to that of any of my challenges.

How amazing would it be if we could create a path that meanders through these woods, wide enough for the kids' wheelchairs to use, so the entire school could experience what it's like to get closer to nature?

The vision I could see in my mind was as real as any painting in front of me, even down to the benches I would have strategically placed in the shade for hot summer days.

'I have got to make this happen,' I thought, driving home like the cat who got the cream.

A couple of weeks later I was back at school with Julie and deputy head Katherine. Estimated costs for the playground and different versions of equipment were unveiled. Totting up the estimates, together with my rough guestimate of around forty thousand pounds for the cost of the woodland path, would reveal the total that I'd need to raise.

Wait for it... drum roll. Drrrrrrrrrrrr.

Yes, you guessed it. Seventy-five thousand pounds!

How ironic?

I walked away from that meeting on a huge high, but also shaking inside and thinking, what the hell have I just agreed to? That was a frightening fortune I'd have to raise. Even though I had never attempted anything on that scale before, I made a silent promise to myself that I would do everything in my power to provide everything the school wanted.

For anyone who's heard of angel numbers, those that you see frequently or repetitively, number seventy-five is a symbolic message to follow your intuition and do not allow others to deter or sway you from your chosen path. Be brave, for the choices you are making are the right ones for you and wonderful new opportunities await. But would all that really unfold?

Priority now was to recruit help from many quarters as I could and get the show on the road.

My first port of call was to contact Dave Poucher, chief photographer at my local newspaper the Rotherham Advertiser, who was already aware of my past and present challenges. Together with Sam Cooper, deputy news editor at that time, I informed them of the latest development. Could we get the publicity that I would surely need underway? As always, I was greeted with the usual enthusiasm and soon the wheels of the press were in motion.

During a trip into Rotherham a couple of weeks later, memories came flooding back as I walked down Wellgate, an area leading to the centre of town, on my way into town for a meeting with a friend. I recalled the first contact I had with Sean Wallage, director of MW Entertainments, a few years earlier when I was trying to attract publicity for my first book *Me and My Shadow*.

As I passed the old shop, now empty, dingy and abandoned, I recalled how the window back then had been attractively set up displaying books and colourful bumf for Help the Heroes, as well as advertising MW Entertainment as agents for a number of famous celebrities.

MW Entertainments no longer occupied the shop, having moved to a new unit on the Magna site on the outskirts of

Rotherham some time ago. But it geared me up to contact Sean again.

The first time we met, it was fate. I would generally walk into town down the left side of Wellgate, but for no apparent reason I had crossed the road this time. Before I knew it, I'd opened the door and there stood Sean. He listened intently to my story without any interruption. I told him of my background and some of the challenges I had successfully taken on over the years in an effort to convince him that the book I had just written was in need of as much publicity as I could get. Could they help?

Yes, they could, and did, taking and selling a good number of books for me.

But could they help me again, this time to address one of my major problems – organising the publicity and media coverage I would undoubtedly need to raise the profile of my 'seventy-five challenge' to subsequently raise such a large amount of money?

'Bear in mind, Sean, this is a charity event and I won't be able to pay for your services. Is there anything you could do to help?' The final question at the end my sales pitch, the like of which I have never delivered before, or since.

Sean agreed to discuss it with his business partner and get back to me, but it sounded promising. We shook hands and I left thinking that the meet had gone well. Fingers crossed.

The next few weeks were non-stop mind blitzing with many sleepless nights, constantly thinking of potential ideas and solutions on how to reach that enormous target.

One of my better ideas was to sell each individual marathon to a main sponsor, their logo emblazoned on the front of my T-shirt as an advertising incentive.

Dominic Hurley, a friend of mine who was much more used to fundraising large amounts of money, had offered to help with the technical side, setting up the seventy-five-date calendar box system on the event website that we had already launched earlier.

The idea was that potential sponsors could log onto the website and choose a particular date, book and pay the price we had set for each marathon. Once booked, that specific date box would then display the sponsor's name with a link to their websites, the date then being unavailable to anyone else.

This system turned out to be a great idea that worked well, once it had been linked to the Golden Giving charity fundraising site which had been one of Sean's early tasks, once MW Entertainment had agreed to become part of the team.

During those early days, it also occurred to me that I would be in desperate need of a personal sponsor to provide the running gear I would undoubtedly need, shoes in particular. The cost of running shoes alone to service the two thousand-plus miles I would be running during the marathons, let alone the even greater number of miles I would be covering during the training leading up to the event, would be mega!

After a constructive meeting with the very knowledgeable Stuart Hale during a visit to Accelerate running store in Attercliffe, Sheffield, I was provided with details of how to contact New Balance, provider of my preferred and current shoe choice.

We agreed that I should be running in familiar shoes during all those miles rather than altering brands to suit any other possible sponsors who would no doubt insist on the change of footwear to publicise their own brand.

As I had been running virtually trouble-free for a good number of years using New Balance 850 and 860 trainers, this made perfect sense.

The following morning, I made the call to their strategic director.

'Hi, my name is Matthews, Ray Matthews. Could I speak to Graham Glasgow, please?'

This name suddenly sounded familiar; a name I began to recall related to a conversation I had had some years previous whilst I was looking for a pair of sand gaiters in readiness for the 100k Del Sahara Desert race. Graham had found and posted a pair to me a few days later and wouldn't even discuss any payment for them. I made full use of the bright red NB gaiters across the Sahara and still have them today! They are a little bit worse for wear now, but you never know when they might come in handy again.

'Hi, Ray, Graham here – what can I do for you?'

'Hi, Graham, I am about to run seventy-five marathons in seventy-five days and wondered if New Balance would care to become involved and help,' I said with enthusiasm.

The line went quiet for a few seconds. 'Really? Tell me about it.'

After a brief explanation of what I felt would help me achieve the challenge he asked if I could make it across to New Balance head office in Warrington for around eleven o'clock the following Tuesday morning.

The days flew by as I was kept busy organising and discussing designs for merchandising that we could sell to help swell the cash that had already started to come in from the marathon sponsors.

During that week, I had also been in discussions with

Dominique Dubreuil, one of the original organisers of our overseas link between Maltby Running Club and the French ACPI (Association des Coureurs du Parc d'Isle) Running Club about taking the fiftieth and fifty-first marathons across the channel to run them in Saint-Quentin.

Of all the places in France, why Saint-Quentin? Well, it just so happens this small town in Aisne, northern France, is twinned with my hometown of Rotherham.

I would need to travel over to Saint-Quentin in plenty of time to discuss the logistics of the two marathons and agreed a date to meet with Dominique in France.

Back to my meeting with New Balance and I set off for Warrington in good time on Tuesday morning, managing a trouble-free journey across the Pennines, arriving pretty much on time.

On arrival, the U-shaped car park at Birchwood looked chock-a-block. But as luck would have it someone was vacating a space fairly close to the New Balance main entrance across the left-hand corner of the unit. I parked up and headed for the double doors with plenty of time to spare.

I was greeted by a familiar-looking athletic guy as I approached the main door. I later realised no wonder he looked familiar; I had been watching him run on a televised cross-country race a few weeks earlier.

He beckoned me to follow as he walked past the main reception desk into a large room dominated by a huge round table around which a group of men were sat waiting.

I felt overwhelmed as I was introduced to them one by one; many of them were talented international runners. Even the Olympics were mentioned during one of the introductions. Wow!

Over a cup of tea, I was invited to sit and explain about the challenge that I had initially mentioned to Graham. All I could think was I was going to have to sell this story big time in order to impress these guys and have them believe that the challenge that I was about to take on would greatly benefit from New Balance's help.

It soon became evident that they were as intrigued about me as I was about these professional athletes seated around me. Facial expressions and body language were the giveaways.

I suppose it wasn't easy for them to take in what they were being told as I ended the shortened version of my running achievements and background over the past few years.

A good number of questions followed but were pitched at me in a friendly, inquisitive manner which needed to be answered with as much of a positive response as I could deliver. I was trying to sell myself, after all.

My answers must have had the desired effect as Graham Glasgow stood up from the table after a good half hour saying he'd have to leave shortly for a pre-arranged meeting. He looked directly at me as he stood up and asked one simple question.

'Ray, will you manage to run seventy-five marathons in seventy-five days?'

Making eye contact, I replied, 'If you can get a bet on it put your house up. It's a cert.'

He smiled and turned to the others. 'Let's give him our support, get him whatever he needs.'

He walked round the table, shook my hand warmly and wished me good luck before leaving the room.

'What's your chest and waist size, and which shoes and size are you using, Ray?' asked Pete Riley, their marketing manager.

I'm a thirty-eight-inch chest, thirty-two-inch waist and size eight and a half shoe. At that time, I was using their 860 V4s. Pete disappeared, leaving me in the company of the New Balance team: David Thompson (who I later learned lived not that far away from me), Bradley Howarth, Andy Parkin and Steve Vernon – all of whom were keen to hear about racing in the Sahara Desert.

But what really intrigued them and caused quite a topic coming as their main question was, 'How is it possible to run 150 miles through two nights without having a sleep?' These guys were so attentive and friendly. I have never felt so welcomed anywhere as I did during that visit to New Balance HQ.

In between our conversations, they were keen to get me in front of the camera doing a photoshoot with them and some of the latest New Balance advertising banners in the background.

Pete finally arrived back, handing me a huge bag full of New Balance kit, minus the shoes, as they didn't have my size in stock at the centre.

Bloody hell! Christmas had come early. Grinning like a Cheshire cat, I said my thanks and goodbyes amid loads of enthusiastic comments from the boys and headed for my car carrying my sack over my shoulders like Father Christmas.

Just over a week later a large cardboard box arrived by courier at my home containing a large quantity of my favourite running shoes. These would last me the rest of my life I reckoned. Who's a lucky boy, then?

Throughout the winter of 2015/16 I started ramping up the training miles, whilst keeping up with the planning and organising of the marathons

Alternating three pairs of my new shoes in a weekly cycle proved to be a formula for success of months of training without any injuries to speak of, other than a tight hamstring close to my right buttock. An old "war wound" complaint that would come and go but sometimes needed a bit of pummelling from expert hands. Those hands belonged to my physiotherapist, Kay Atkin of Pure Physiotherapy, who always put me back on the right track again.

Pure Physiotherapy had been a big part of my successful running challenges over the years, with me having initially been looked after by Phin Robinson, founder and owner of the rapidly expanding physiotherapy clinics. Phin, who had provided invaluable expert treatment, had moved to live in Norfolk but had agreed to come on board and offer their full support as part of the seventy-five marathons team. I would be relying on Kay to repair any damage that I would inevitably pick up during the two and a half months of consecutive daily marathons, as well as all those thousands of miles of training. Did she realise what she was taking on?

The team was coming together nicely; all was going well and taking shape. Having sorted out the sponsors with the help of I-Motion gym for the seventy-five individual T-shirts, the last pieces of the jigsaw were coming together. These shirts, sponsored by the huge Danish sports company Hummel, easily recognisable by the four chevrons down the sleeves, arrived in a large box at the gym which also included tracksuits, shorts, socks and light running tops. Fabulous. Just what the doctor ordered. I had enough kit now to set up a shop!

The next step was my upcoming meeting in Saint-Quentin.

Late February 2016, my suitcase packed, I set off for

France. Travelling by car via Eurostar with Sean Rogers. Sean, one of the original members of Manvers Running Club who was helping organise the seventy-five marathons challenge, had agreed to join me in France. From what I had been able to glean from Dominique, a main sponsor in Saint-Quentin was looking forward to meeting us.

We arrived late afternoon and booked into Hotel Le Florence, close to the town centre. Early next morning after breakfast we were met in reception by Dominique and the ACPI Running Club chairman, Jean-Claude Lerche, with the usual French greeting of a kiss on both cheeks.

I had met Dominique and Jean-Claude on many occasions as we, the Maltby Running Club members, had exchanged visits over a number of years to take part in events in the UK and France and had become good friends.

We were whisked away to attend a pre-arranged meeting with the town's most influential newspaper to provide all the details of the marathons I was about to take on and why two marathons would see us coming to Saint-Quentin. The publicity I was hoping for could help attract more sponsorship whilst in France.

Dominique provided the interpretation – with a few choice words from Jean-Claude – during the meeting with the paper's editor and reporters, which lasted for a good two hours.

Back to our hotel for a spot of lunch, during which time a detailed description of the routes was discussed. All the routes had already been worked out and Jean-Claude assured me that each day's marathon would be an accurate 42.2km.

A 9am start at the Parc d'Isle was also suggested as the routes would take in the canal towpath and surrounding villages. From memory of running part of these areas the previous year, I was more than pleased with his choice. This would make for a very picturesque and pleasant couple of days' running. An early start meant I would cross the finish line soon before the high afternoon temperatures of August hit – good thinking, Jean-Claude.

I was also informed about a sponsor they had managed to secure. Dominique would provide their company logo that we would print on two T-shirts. It was also insinuated that ACPI would do some fundraising before and during our weekend stay.

It would be a very demanding and intense weekend in August – I had no doubt of that. But it would be more than worth all the effort we would have to put in to successfully pull this one off.

We said our goodbyes and headed for home, pleased with the overall outcome of our flying visit.

How ironic that at the time of writing this account of the story, England are playing France in the Six Nations Rugby Union Championship on TV. England won – sorry, my French friends, but you were trounced!

Anyway, I digress. It was now late April and I was running six days a week, averaging around fifteen miles a day and getting ready to increase the training up to twenty miles a day, seven days a week before backing off a couple of weeks before the challenge began.

I had planned to start the first marathon on my seventy-fifth birthday, 30th June, but we decided to move it on two days as that year the 30th fell on a Thursday. A midweek start would not be great to provide the highest impact this challenge deserved. Saturday 2nd July was chosen as the official start date and agreed by all.

My fitness was at last really beginning to show as I was now comfortably running twenty miles each day. I reckoned adrenaline would enable me to run the extra miles needed to complete the 26.2 minimum miles every day for seventy-five days. I also figured that I would be running myself into a super-fit state within no time at all, carrying very few surplus pounds, which I would shed long before the challenge began.

Most of our local running clubs had finally become involved and were very supportive of my challenge, having pre-booked and sponsored many marathons. All I needed to do was just turn up each day and run a measured pre-set route in either Rotherham, Sheffield, around South Yorkshire, Lincolnshire, Derbyshire or the West Midlands.

At this stage most of the seventy-five marathons had been allocated and paid for in one way or another. As the start date drew nearer I was getting increasingly more excited. I was so looking forward to running the marathons, either solo or surrounded by running colleagues.

It would soon be time to put all the months of training, negotiating and planning into action and literally 'get the show on the road'.

*

Guest Contribution

Dave Poucher, chief photographer, *Rotherham Advertiser*

Among the many happy stand-out memories I have of Dave, who always seemed to be present come rain or shine during my many challenges, was our photo session around Roche

Abbey. We had spent hours taking action photos of me for my book Who Dares *and especially the dramatic action shots whilst racing across the stream, creating fountains of water. Dave is a much-appreciated supporter and friend.*

Ray Matthews

I first met Ray on a sunny afternoon whilst looking to do some photographs for his second book at Roche Abbey in Rotherham. Little did I know the journey it was about to take me on over the next few years.

Ray is the kind of person you can become instantly friends with: softly spoken, polite but most of all a true gent. You soon learn that if he says he is going to do something then it gets done and he will put his heart and soul into making sure it does no matter what barriers are thrown up against him.

This became obvious when he told me about his seventy-five-marathon challenge to raise money to build a new all-weather play area at Newman School, which then went on to include a nature track around the school grounds and a swimming pool, as you do.

At first, I took a look at him and thought he was joking. Surely no mere mortal could run seventy-five marathons in seventy-five days at seventy-five years of age. I got a sweat on just running the bath! But, of course, Ray is no mere mortal and within weeks we were doing promo pics of him pounding the streets in preparation for what he called a birthday present to himself. Madness!

His herculean efforts took him to every corner of the borough and beyond, he even completed two marathons in France. I remember waving him off in Maltby with his team of supporters, knowing in less than forty-eight hours he would be back on the streets of Rotherham continuing his challenge on home soil.

Of course, he smashed it and raised a staggering total for Newman School in the process. I will never forget covering the day when he finished his task and crossed the line on the seventy-fifth day, with the Mayor of Rotherham stood shouting and whooping at him, surrounded by friends, supporters and most importantly children from Newman School (where he is now a god), cheering him on. You couldn't not feel a sense of pride and admiration for the man.

After completing this task, Ray, being Ray, needed another focus and before long the telephone was ringing with an excited voice saying, 'Dave, I've got something for you, we are going to get the schools of Rotherham running a mile a day to promote health and wellbeing. What do you think?'

Didn't really matter what I thought, as I knew it would happen, and sure enough after a few weeks' planning, my colleagues and I were visiting different schools around the borough taking pictures of excited schoolchildren pounding the playgrounds, come rain or snow, but more importantly loving every yard of it. Another tick on the Ray Matthews things-to-do list.

As part of this challenge, he hooked up with St Bede's Primary School and helped with fundraising and planning to get a purpose-built all-weather running track and football pitch built in an old yard. This now looks superb and allows the children to carry on their daily exercise routine which has proved so beneficial to so many pupils.

In between all of this, he became an ambassador for the charity Age UK Rotherham, where he helped raise awareness of the crippling effects of loneliness and the mental health issues it can cause within the elderly community and vulnerable social groups. He did this by setting up special drop-in centres at supermarkets and community centres to get his message across, which again was a great success.

He also helped kick-start the Rotherham 10K race which had become mothballed for years. This was so much of a success with hundreds taking part and raising big chunks of money for Age UK; his team couldn't wait to make it bigger and better the following year.

Then the coronavirus pandemic struck and everything came to a grinding halt, with schools shutting and people finding the new norm, sitting at home, unable to see family and friends. This drew even more attention to Ray's campaign against loneliness and helping people reach out to get through what became unprecedented times. Most of us sat back and battened down the hatches and waited for it to run its course, but not Ray. He decided that it would be a good idea to get people out doing their own virtual 10K or whatever they could manage. From babies in prams to pensioners on Zimmer frames, the take-up was immense and, of course, the Virtual 10K became a huge success.

Ray was awarded the British Citizen award and also nominated for a Pride of Britain award (should have won it – he was robbed!) and even popped into Buckingham Palace. Luckily he managed to curb his enthusiasm and didn't get the whole royal party running around the grounds, although I'm sure the thought crossed his mind!

He is now a bit of a local celebrity and when he is not opening the local village fete or giving an inspiring talk to schoolchildren and adults alike on the importance of health and mental wellbeing, he may be just out enjoying a casual run with a hundred-plus excited schoolchildren and staff blazing a trail behind him, desperately trying to beat him to the finish line.

I can truly say that we will be friends for life now and I am sure it won't be long before my mobile rings and I see the screen saying 'Ray Matthews' calling and I wonder what on earth he is going to do now!

3

From the Red Lion to Phoenix

If the next challenge you dream about taking on doesn't scare the living daylights out of you, it's probably nowhere near big enough to ignite that flame.

Passion, discipline, positivity and hard work, with a modicum of talent, has been the formula for any success that I have achieved and enjoyed over the years since I made that life-changing decision to become a boxer.

Benny Kemp, my first boxing coach and mentor, provided the foundation all those years ago for a way of life that I have found both challenging and rewarding in equal quantities. His patience, understanding and teachings formed the basics I would need throughout my life.

Over the short time we were together, my patient coach taught me how to activate self-motivation and how to get the best out of me. He taught me about discipline, respect and how to control emotions. He also taught me how to ignite passion and, above all, the ability to analyse and rationally make decisions of importance both in and out of the ring.

Towards the end of our two years together we had discussed the need for me to move on from the Red Lion to a more progressive club in order to further advance my career. Benny suggested I join the best boxing club in the area at that time, the Phoenix Boxing Club, which was part of the large steel manufacturing company Steel, Peech and Tozer, where no less than seven ABA (Amateur Boxing Association) champions trained and fought from.

'You'll soon be twelve, Ray. It's a good time to move on and get a foot on the ladder and unfortunately it's something I can't give you,' he said.

Before my last training session at the Red Lion had started, Benny took me to one side with his arm around my shoulder, but this time, rather than him steering me towards the ring, we were heading towards the door.

'Grab your bag and come with me.'

With a heavy heart, guessing what was about to happen, I was taken down to "Steelos", as it was lovingly known by all the boxing club members, I later found out. We boarded the number 69 bus just a hundred yards away on Corporation Street opposite from the Odeon cinema and made our way, in silence, out of the town down Sheffield Road to Ickles.

Trepidation mixed with the excitement of what was happening created an overwhelming desire to run as we left the bus.

After entering this impressive large open building on Sheffield Road, I stood there with kit bag in hand being introduced to this giant of a man who had been instructing a couple of young lads in the ring. He now stood facing me with an outstretched hand for me to shake.

'Hello, Ray, I'm Jacky Pearson,' he said. I was a bag of

nerves and shaking like a leaf, trying to control my emotions whilst I was being introduced to my new coach.

I managed a sheepish hello and shook his large hand, with a sickening feeling that I was being handed over like a little orphan to Mr Pearson, for want of better words.

'You will be joining one of the most successful boxing clubs in South Yorkshire if you come to us,' he said.

Mr Pearson was aware of who I was; our paths had crossed during my début fight in my first outdoor exhibition bout in the Red Lion Square when I fought against one of his boys a couple of months after I had made that initial 'I wanna be a boxer' statement.

Jacky Pearson welcomed me with open arms and, right from the start, I was made to feel at home as he walked me round the gym and changing room. We hit it off immediately which helped to lessen the feelings I was having of being abandoned, even though I had understood Benny's motives as he waved and headed for the door. I never saw him again.

I will never forget Benny Kemp. From such a young age I had grown so attached to one of the most endearing, influential men in my life. Although he is no longer alive, I often hear his voice when I need inspiration, guidance or advice during long challenges that become, let's say, challenging!

My new coach, an ex-Royal Navy boxing champion and physical training instructor, insisted on nothing but the best from all his fighters – without exception.

Jacky imposed a brutal training programme right from the start during my twice-weekly, two and a half-hour training sessions at the gym – which soon became five-days-a-week training for me. I likened it to the military discipline you would have expected in the forces.

This new way of training had almost instant results. Over the next eighteen months or so as I successfully progressed from my first fight to my fortieth in less time that it takes to say, 'I love boxing.'

I had become an apprentice of a great tutor and soon had my feet placed firmly on the ladder. My boxing career had really begun.

It was during this time when running became an important part of my training, regularly clocking up between ten and fourteen miles a day, five days a week, before and after school as a means of building up stamina. I must admit, I honestly hated running then with as much passion as I love it today!

The yin and yang within me was now in sync. I was much less confrontational and able to control the temper that a couple of years previously would have erupted like a volcano over a simple childish comment like someone calling me ginger. Life was easier at school for both teachers and classmates alike. Mum was also relieved that I had become more likely to stay out of trouble. I was 'becoming dependable', I remember she had commented.

As I look back and reflect, the two most significant decisions and hardest lessons in my life happened before my fourteenth birthday, and both to do with boxing.

The first, as you already know, was to pluck up the courage to visit the Red Lion Pub and say yes to becoming a boxer. The second came on one cold November evening in Leicester during my fiftieth fight, this time against a National Coal Board champion, where I completely lost the plot.

I am not proud to admit, and it's still hard to write about the fact that, even all those years ago, I completely abused the code of conduct and teachings that had been instilled in me from both Benny and then Jacky, when I arrogantly decided to play about for the first two rounds with an opponent who clearly lacked the skills I had been used to fighting against, and then knock him out in the third.

I was unbeatable, or so I misguidedly thought, and my plan to bring the fight to an end before the final bell in the last round didn't happen as I finally chased him around the ring trying to land the knockout blow.

Through sheer arrogance and big-headedness, my unbeaten record came to a disastrous end. I lost my fiftieth fight.

Jacky was fuming to say the least, using language that I had never heard from him before or since as we left the ring after that farcical episode. As we stepped into the dressing room, even before I had time to apologise I was told to keep my mouth shut, with him clearing the dressing room of our young boxers. I was then on the receiving end of the biggest dressing-down I had ever experienced – the like of which I have thankfully never had to endure since.

I was told not to come to the gym for a couple of weeks, in order to reflect on my arrogance and improper unsportsmanlike conduct.

Two tormented weeks later, and whilst fearing the worst, knowing what was in front of me, I forced myself to confront my feelings and go back to the gym where I was subjected to the most humbling experience ever.

I was made to stand in the centre of the ring, like a criminal in the dock, after Jacky had met me at the door and then cleared a couple of young lads who had been sparring in the ring.

He escorted me into the ring and afforded me the opportunity to apologise to the whole club, officials and parents for my arrogant misgivings, an experience I never wanted to repeat as everyone stopped what they had been doing and stood in silence, listening to my humble apology.

I had expected that my lack of discipline, respect and total disregard for everything I had been taught would have brought an early end to my boxing career with this great club.

But Jacky forgave me. 'It's character-building and you had the guts to apologise under the most difficult conditions. I am proud of you,' he said half an hour later.

We moved on from that experience with a powerful reserve that I would never put myself in that position ever again. Lesson well and truly learned.

Plain sailing would be a good description of my life shortly after that episode as the familiarity of hard training and incident-free school life had become the norm.

Well, it was until that evening arrived a few months before my fifteenth birthday when I was introduced to Danny, a visiting professional flyweight from Ireland, who arrived at our gym during one of my midweek training sessions.

Professionals were often invited to train at our gym. It gave us an insight into the world of the professional methods of training and fighting.

I thought I knew how to box; in my amateur boxing world, I had become content and naïvely satisfied.

Danny turned that misguided illusion upside-down within just twelve minutes of our first sparring session in the ring. I was made to feel like a Christian martyr in the Colosseum trying to avoid becoming the lion's next meal, as I encountered my first real boxing lesson since I had started.

I soon realised that I wasn't anywhere near skilled or fit enough to be in the same ring as my professional sparring partner.

What a rude awakening I had during those first three rounds.

The difference between amateur and professional boxing is chasms apart as I was forced to find out the hard way, using pure instinct for survival, during that first encounter in the ring with Danny.

It would have been easy to have backed away and have chosen to continue with an illusion that I was good enough in my cosy amateur boxing world.

The decision had to be made. Should I take advantage of this golden opportunity that had suddenly presented itself and learn how to box like a pro and make a giant leap with new skills? It would be hard, I had no doubt about that, but the rewards would be enormous.

'Let's go for it,' I decided.

The choice I made that evening, against my dad's wishes, I might add, for me to continue sparring and learn from my new teacher turned out to be one of the greatest decisions I have ever made.

There would be around three months of available time to learn from this extremely talented professional before he would be heading back to Ireland in preparation for his upcoming European title fight in France.

To save any interruption to my new schooling, I had requested that my name was taken out of being available for competition whilst I was training with Danny.

Week after week of hard work and dedication with my new sparring partner eventually culminated in a successful, satisfactory conclusion as our sparring sessions became less one-sided. I was starting to hold my own and was actually beginning to contribute more to the once one-sided partnership.

I was actually now enjoying our intense sparring sessions which had been increased in time and duration to suit Danny's up-and-coming championship fight.

Danny had provided me with the opportunity that few boys of my age could ever dream about, let alone experience the skills that I was being taught during our time together. We became great friends and worked well together, bouncing off each other to become fight-ready and even fitter than I could ever imagine.

It was like saying goodbye to a big brother as we shook hands and hugged one another for the very last time before he departed back to Ireland.

Danny left with a parting comment that not only surprised but spurred me on to do even better.

'Ray, you're becoming dangerously close to being good.' High praise indeed from the next European featherweight champion.

'I can and will do better.'

*

Even though my name had been taken off the available list for any inter-club competitions during the time I had spent with Danny, I had been happy to devote my entire time and attention to acquiring the new skills I was being taught in our twice-weekly sessions together. We had also spent hours cross-country running up and around Kimberworth and Costhorpe, which worked well from his hotel, the Prince of Wales, just opposite the old Masbrough Railway Station.

Shortly after Danny's departure I was summoned, during a training session, to a conversation that was taking place in the gym between Jacky and the club's manager-promoter, Jack Cox.

I would soon have the opportunity to put my new skills into practice, I was being told. An invite had arrived from a Liverpool promoter asking for our club to provide nine or ten boxers to take on a mixed represented club fighters from Liverpool and across the north of England, even as far as Scotland.

Liverpool has always been renowned for quality fighters and, from the description of an opponent I was being matched up with, this was one of them.

Many knockouts (KOs) and technical knockouts (TKOs) were registered under his name and read like a horror story to any would-be opponent.

'Just what we're looking for, a great chance to test out your new skills,' Jacky said. I would no doubt have to meet him anyway if I progressed beyond the Yorkshire Schoolboy championship to the Northern County championships in a few months' time.

A code of practice existed back then between club coaches and managers to supply accurate factual accounts of fighters who they were trying to match up so that a mismatch didn't occur. It didn't always work out like that and in this case I was under no illusion that they would more than likely have understated than exaggerated my next opponent's impressive record.

Time marches on and before I knew it, I was stood in this impressive hall situated on the outskirts of Liverpool, looking across from my dressing room at the large, elevated ring in the centre of the biggest arenas I had ever had the opportunity to fight in.

I was gearing up ready to make that long walk down the avenue of seats, through the local crowd to the ring, having just watched with pride as our three younger boxers kick-started this event. They had outperformed their opponents with wins for two and a decision that could have gone either way but went to the opposition for the other.

It was my turn to feel that exhilaration again that only boxing has ever provided as I walked, as usual, with Jacky's large hands on my shoulders, all the way down the avenue of seated boxing fans and, after climbing the few steps, 'elegantly' entered this full-size ring into the blue corner.

I waited for my opponent to arrive amidst chants of 'Sammy, Sammy, Sammy' echoing around this large hall from the enthusiastic partisan crowd. The hall seemed to be packed to the brim with his followers.

I could sense the air was filled with anticipation of the inevitable outcome the crowd would be expecting. If his record and past performances had anything to go by, I was about to become his next victim.

I had become used to this behaviour from supporters; it's always been an additional pleasure, upsetting the locals, but this Liverpool crowd were not aware of my secret weapon – Danny.

I was here on a double mission full of determination to put the ghost of my fiftieth fight to rest and chomping at the bit to put my new skills to work, eager to get the fight underway.

My opponent, unusually, didn't look in my direction as he entered the ring. Even when the referee brought us together in the middle of the ring, he avoided eye contact with me, kept his head bowed and just nodded at the referee's instructions.

Slightly smaller, I estimated, but stockier than me with close-cropped dark hair was my first impression of this Liverpudlian, who still hadn't looked in my direction as we retreated back to our corners in readiness to do battle.

'You're going to have to look at me soon,' I was thinking as the bell sounded for the first round.

What followed was the most explosive start I have ever seen from any of my opponents. He came thundering towards me with fists flying even before he got near me.

This stocky, powerful-looking opponent looked as though he'd been catapulted out of his corner.

I'd hardly had time to move away from my corner but managed to side-step and catch him with a good right-hander before he sailed past, almost crashing into my corner.

Should I have been surprised by this violent start? No, I shouldn't. This was obviously how he had managed to win with so many KOs, charging at his opponents like a rampant bull!

Quite clearly his intentions were to intimidate, but fortunately for me, although he possessed the power and probably the mindset of a winner, he lacked the skills or the fitness because within a minute of this aggressive pattern, he was breathing heavily and showing early signs of tiredness.

A lull in his attack and him quickly tiring was making it easier for me to catch him with some telling blows. I was content to score points and just out-box him for the remainder of the round.

I was happy with my overall performance as round one came to an end with me on top but still very much aware of the punching power he clearly possessed.

Round two followed pretty much the same pattern, with an explosive start from him, sending the partisan crowd into a frenzy of chanting his name. However, once again I was able to use the skills that I had spent months learning from Danny to take control using reaction speed to evade his powerful swinging punches.

I was back on top again shortly after the start of round two and able to link some good combination punches together. This provides the flowing movements that sets up the continuity, as each punch delivered provided the perfect opening to deliver the next punch from a spot-on position.

Towards the middle of the round, he was again rapidly tiring and back-pedalling trying to avoid punches that were getting through. I was now connecting with a good amount of telling punches without much resistance.

He was controllable and I was winning, but towards the end of the round, whilst I had him bent double in a corner scoring heavily, without warning he violently jumped up and outwards, headbutting me just over my left eye.

Stars of all shapes, sizes and colour exploded in my head and, whilst expecting the ref to intervene, I rapidly backed away, anticipating that the blood would start flowing at any second. It didn't, but I could feel the swelling erupting almost immediately. Amazingly, no reprimand from the referee.

'What the…?!'

As the round came to an end, I hotfooted it back to my corner, where Jacky, now inside the ring, grabbed and sat me down in one fell swoop.

Whilst he worked on the swelling with the miniature iron trying to reduce the swelling, the referee sauntered over and asked if I would be able to continue, which convinced me that the swelling must look pretty severe. Jacky complained bitterly about the headbutt, which seemed to fall on deaf ears as he turned away from us and took up a position in a neutral corner.

Hell's bells! I was not only fighting my opponent, who hadn't had the decency to acknowledge his misdemeanour, but also the ref and crowd as well!

'If you're happy to continue, you're going to have to finish this one early,' Jacky said. I nodded in acknowledgement. 'Tire him out then get it over with before you're stopped by the ref.'

Incredibly I was not in any pain but conscious of the swelling that was slowly increasing in size. Thankfully, I was still able to see clearly enough as the bell sounded for the last round.

I was on a mission now, using my left hand to hide the swelling from the ref whenever he was on my left side so he couldn't get a good look at my damaged eye.

Fortunately, I was able to control Sammy from the start and at the same time keep the referee behind me, but time was running out. I was becoming more and more desperate; my eye was now almost closed and I was worried that a premature end was imminent.

Upping the level of attack and throwing all caution to the wind with a non-stop barrage of heavy-scoring punches was working; the long hours of running and training with Danny was paying dividends.

Midway through the round, when my opponent was

on his last legs, an opportunity to back him onto the ropes presented itself as I punched him hard in the stomach and, through tiredness, he came bouncing back off the ropes like a rag doll onto the sweetest of right-handers I had ever delivered. I knew instantly before he hit the canvas that he wasn't going to get up from that one. Sometimes you just know.

I was almost dragged, as I stood over him, to a neutral corner by the referee and watched the proceedings out of my good eye. My opponent, who lay face-down and hadn't moved, was being worked on by his team who had jumped into the ring to his aid even before the referee had started counting.

The fight doctor was sent for as his two corner men turned him over onto his side and removed his gum shield, splashing water onto his face from a laden sponge.

Sammy looked in distress and hadn't moved by himself.

This is the unpleasant part of boxing that does have an effect on me.

Looking out from the ring, using my good eye, I could sense the concern of the now-quiet crowd as the bright overhead ring lights seemed to be scorching the top of my head. I couldn't wait to leave the ring.

A good five minutes later he was helped onto his seat by his two corner men and the doctor. It was another few more minutes before Sammy was able to stand.

I could see the bluey-red mark just above the left side of his lower jaw, a bit higher than where I thought I had connected.

The result was shortly announced and we left the ring almost together.

After showering off, the doctor arrived and spent some

time inspecting my damaged eye. Jacky had suggested that it may be a good idea to nick the swelling in order to release the pressure, but the doctor reckoned that it wouldn't be beneficial and delivered a further blow that it would take a good six weeks or so to heal.

My eye was all the colours of the rainbow by now and well and truly closed. I was sporting a proper boxing trophy for the first time!

During the doctor's eye inspection, I discovered that my opponent had been taken home by his parents shortly after leaving the ring. I would be public enemy number one, I expected.

The dull pain around my eye was starting to multiply with every minute and I was becoming increasingly more upset with the doctor's comment of how long my eye would take to heal. But, worse still, I wasn't looking forward to walking in at home and upsetting Mum. In those days, there was no way that I could pre-warn her by sending a selfie on the coach home.

I was due to fight in the Yorkshire championships in just over four weeks' time. Do miracles ever happen in real life, I wondered? I certainly needed one if I was to make it there.

Mum and Dad survived the initial shock and, after a couple of days off school, I was able to continue training, without any sparring, of course. As the swelling slowly decreased it was confirmed that around half an inch of bone had broken away from the brow.

It's still a trophy I can feel today, as I write about that time of my life.

I wore my colourful, swollen eye around my mates like a hard-earned winner's medal. But, at the same time,

I was concerned that, with only two weeks to go until the championships, the swelling and colour didn't look good at all. I resigned myself to the inevitable. I would be in no fit state, medically, to fight for the Yorkshire schoolboy title.

During a midweek training session, the start of the miracle was about to happen. Whilst knocking hell out of the large bag, I was approached by an old guy whom I had occasionally noticed in the gym. He used to visit on a fairly regular basis at one time and would sit and watch us training for hours.

'That's a nasty-looking eye, young 'un,' he said, coming closer to fully inspect my war wound. 'You need to get some Oil of Origanum on that. It will clear the swelling and shift the bruise. Be gone in a couple of weeks.' Whilst giving me instructions on how to apply the oil, he also emphasised just how much it was going to sting.

I was starting to feel optimistic, especially after Jacky informed me how respected and much sought after this old guy was in the fight business. It turned out that he was a well-known professional cornerman, more than capable of dealing with cuts and damaged eyes.

I couldn't wait to get home to tell Mum and Dad, and hopefully get a bottle as soon as possible to start the treatment.

Amazingly, it worked! After just a few days the swelling was already disappearing fast and the colour was less prominent – and it blinking well did sting! But my new worry was, what if the championship doctor happened to be the same one that had seen the damage at Liverpool?

The Saturday morning of the Yorkshire championships arrived and our team of six fighters had an early trip to a large hall, somewhere in the centre of Leeds.

We needed to be at the event centre in time to check in, weigh in and get through the medical for the first of the possible couple of elimination fights that would take place during the afternoon before, if successful, the final fight during the evening.

I had received a final facial makeover from Mum before leaving home, using her foundation cream, powder and rouge to camouflage and hide the last of the discolouration.

Who thinks that was cheating? Well, I didn't think so. I felt justified remembering all the long hours of training.

I made out that it didn't hurt; it was the only way I could get Mum and Dad to allow me to fight in this tournament – never mind forgetting to mention that I would probably be taking part in at least three bouts if I progressed through to the final.

Although still somewhat tender to touch, I hoped and even prayed it looked good enough to fool the doctor.

I was feeling more relaxed and my nerves settled down once I had seen that this event doctor was not the same one as the doctor at the Liverpool event.

Weigh-in was a different kettle of fish, though. I came in four ounces over the limit and couldn't believe it because it was something of a ritual before fights that we were all weighed at the gym in time to make final adjustments in order to hit the desired target weight at tournament weigh-in.

With no other option available, Jacky suggested that I could sweat it off given that I had over an hour and a half to meet the deadline.

Four ounces probably seems an insignificant amount to lose for most; it's about the weight of a pack of cards. But when you're lean and don't carry an ounce of fat on your body, it became an uphill task. It took a good hour of hard skipping wearing as many clothes as I could physically get on – even a bulky camel-coloured duffel coat was added to help break a sweat.

Two trips to the toilet, finger and toenails clipped, and even a hasty close-cropped haircut, which looked as though a knife and fork had been used, finally resulted in the desired eight stone and a little bit requirement with only five minutes to spare.

What I can never understand is the fact that you can make the weight on the limit, and then you can go out and stuff your face to bursting, which would take you well overweight.

The two afternoon eliminations bouts, after luckily receiving a 'bye' in the first rounds, went well, with me managing to coast through both fights without taking too much out of the tank. Jacky's instructions were to just do enough to win and protect my eye, which meant that I would be as strong a possible for the championship bout later that evening.

I had plenty of time to rest and fuel up for the evening's fight, which was scheduled for around 8pm.

I had already come across and beaten my final opponent on points eight or nine months ago. I felt relaxed and comfortable, looking forward to my last fight of the day.

The hall was packed out for the evening's bouts with wall-to-wall seated noisy boxing fans that could be heard even all the way back to my dressing room.

Steelos were having a great night so far, with all our fighters taking the win and crowned Yorkshire champions – no more than I would have expected from some of the most talented fighters in the country.

My turn arrived at just a few minutes after eight when Jacky arrived at the dressing room door.

'Let's go,' he mouthed.

I was already in the zone, having had plenty of time to reflect whilst waiting for my fight to come round. I had been through my strategy for the fight a few times in my head as I had relaxed for over an hour and a half, laid out on a wooden bench, and with eyes closed, I was able to recall our previous match at the Southey Green Working Men's Club in Sheffield.

But does the strategy in your head always work in reality? The elements of someone else's influence need to be accounted for in that dream. Well, on this occasion my aspirations became a reality, proving that dreams really can come true.

During the fight I had managed to avoid any contact to my eye other than when we came together in a clinch during the last round, which produced a sharp reminder of the Liverpool episode.

I was more than delighted with my performance, which resulted in a resounding win and a huge grin from Jacky, who I'm sure would have felt my pain and jumped into action should I have been punched on my still-damaged eye.

Proud parents and excited brothers greeted me on my arrival home as I was able to, with a deserved degree of bragging rights, show the gleaming White Yorkshire Rose cloth badge that I could proudly attach to my competition shorts.

Month after month I continued to fight all over the country, sometimes three or four times a month, with a continued successful winning streak taking my tally of over one hundred fights to a new club record.

Most of my fights during the next couple of years I vaguely

remember, but without any real incidents worth mentioning other than all had gone smoothly and according to plan.

But it did occur to me that all of a sudden I was fighting much less frequently as time went by. Success has its disadvantages, it seems, as the only opportunity to take part in tournaments came from far-away cities and counties. So, as long as I was prepared to travel, there was a steady enough flow of opponents to keep me from becoming completely stale.

Of late, I was being matched against boxers who were looking to take scalps and further advance their own careers, and on occasions, whilst competing miles away from home, I was the only boxer representing the Phoenix Boxing Club.

Training alone was nowhere nearly enough to satisfy my hunger. I needed to compete and fight competitively in the ring.

4
Nipples of steel

'Morning, Ray, how's thi nipples?'

'Are we allowed to talk about nipples on live radio, Rony?'

'You can on my show, my friend,' came back the reply as quick as you like in that deep, rasping voice I had become so accustomed to.

I could never tell what this very popular funny guy was likely to ask next and a question like that had been typical over the past few years.

'OK then, Rony, I have nipples of steel,' I replied, trying to sound serious, forcing myself not to burst out laughing whilst trying to imagine what the non-runners in our listeners were thinking at this opening comment during our now-weekly chat.

He'd obviously been talking to a runner since we last spoke, I suspected.

My nipples are fine and have been for a good few years since first experiencing that bloodied vest and very painful chapel hat peg nipples during a long, hot, sunny training run. I remember it well, when the blood from my nipples mixed with copious amounts of sweat made my running vest look like I had just escaped from the slaughterhouse. You can imagine the strange looks I got from everyone I passed.

Runner's nipples are well documented and occur with the chafing of sweat-soaked vests; it occurs when the constant movement between the vest and skin causes friction and a great deal of soreness which usually ends in bleeding, if not treated by some form of lubrication.

I soon learned that a light dab of Vaseline gave me all the protection I needed and now I don't have that problem, so long as I remember to put it on. Otherwise, it's a removed vest part-way during the run and take on that half-naked look to complete the run.

'What are you doing tomorrow, Ray?'

I think he had meant to ask, 'Where are you running tomorrow, Ray?', but I couldn't resist the classic reply.

'I'll be running, Rony. Running,' I answered.

But quick as a flash he replied, 'That's great, Forrest. Where are you now, my friend?'

These first few questions from Rony Robinson in our regular weekly Monday morning live interviews on BBC Radio Sheffield were as unrehearsed as ever and often took me by surprise.

Prior to our live slot, Rony's researcher or studio manager would make contact with me at a pre-arranged time, usually around 10am, generally a few minutes before we were due to go live. I would be asked not to move once they had a 'fix' on me.

Hell's bells! Big Brother was watching me – could they actually latch on to my location?

'I am running across a field,' I replied.

'Describe where you are, Ray.'

'Well, I am on a wide path running between two corn fields heading out towards the village of Woodsetts and in the distance I can see some large trees across the skyline on the edge of the village.

'There's also a gaggle of buzzards hovering above waiting for me to drop.'

Didn't know if that's the right name for the birds, but it just came out.

I wasn't kidding either. I had just noticed high above in a cloudless blue sky this "wake" of about ten buzzards gliding effortless in a never-ending circle above me like a scene from a desert documentary. They appeared to be waiting for their next meal to give up the ghost – me!

'Best keep moving then, Ray,' was Rony's comment.

We discussed over the next ten minutes or so how I was feeling, how the marathons were panning out and how the fundraising was going and talked about the plans I had for the coming week. Then the music kicked in, signalling our talk had come to the end of live transmission.

'That went well, Ray. Look after yourself and we will catch up next Monday, around the same time. I will give your website and JustGiving page a mention or two later. Ta-ra.'

I loved our regular new Monday morning live chats, which were very much different to some of the past invited studio interviews that took place, sitting in the soundproofed room in Shoreham Street, Sheffield.

Our light-hearted weekly chats were becoming a huge hit, I was informed, with an ever-growing audience in and around the South Yorkshire catchment area. They were massively helping me to get the fundraising message out to a wider area. I was, after all, trying to raise a staggering seventy-five thousand pounds. But these chats had also became a weekly relaxed interlude from the very serious challenge I'd set myself.

As I set off running towards Woodsetts on the outskirts of Nottinghamshire, the image of our last live studio interview, some weeks before the seventy-five-marathon challenge got underway, came flooding back.

Rony and I had spent a few minutes during his morning show talking about my previous 100km twenty-four-hour challenge, where I had accompanied Kerry Levins, a blind ex-serviceman, from London to Brighton. We ran over the South Downs through the night to raise much-needed funds for Blind Veterans UK. During the interview we did a live link with Kerry whilst he was receiving physio treatment on a long-standing injury.

Our interviews were always light-hearted and full of fun but still managed to get the serious message over as we briefly talked about boxing, where it had all started, together with some of the running events and the latest upcoming marathon challenge in an effort to provide some media coverage to boost our fundraising target.

At the conclusion to this, the last interview before the start of the first marathon, Rony had suggested we have our photo taken together for further media output at the end of our live session.

Interview finished, studio sound off and music switched to automatic play, one of the researchers entered Rony's soundproof studio with camera in hand to take our photo together.

As I turned towards him, he suddenly surprised me by

stripping to the waist and invited me to do the same, stating, 'I'll show thi mine if thy'll show me thine,' with a huge cheeky grin on his unshaven face.

I dare say nothing ever surprised me about this guy, but the sight of his sixty-odd-year-old torso – and how much more he was going to expose – did.

Once I realised that was as far as he was going, I peeled off my top and we stood at the back of the studio posing like a couple of prize fighters in the Marquess of Queensbury stance, squaring up to one another for the photo. Luckily it's only live radio and not TV.

The photo became an overnight global hit on the world media circuit.

When I saw it for the first time, it all made sense and why it had caused so much attention.

With not a lot of imagination, we looked as though we were both posing bollock-naked, with the sound desk coming to the rescue, cutting the bottom half of our torsos from view. It still makes me laugh.

Back to our Monday morning marathon.

I was heading out to Turnerwood, which for me is one of the most picturesque little villages you could find anywhere in the country. The village is dominated by the frequently used Chesterfield canal with limestone bungalows and a row of quaint terraced stone houses that once housed railway workers and local Anston Quarry men.

The stone from this quarry, just over a mile away, which was shipped down the canal in huge blocks, was used to build the upper part of the Houses of Parliament.

I was running comfortably, feeling good and looking forward to seeing my friend Diane Gleeson around midday, where I intended to have a short break at her little summerhouse cafe, Orchard Teas, on the edge of the canal. I'd catch up with the latest gossip and eat my bread and blackcurrant jam sandwiches before heading down the towpath into Worksop.

Diane would enthusiastically introduce me to her customers like the host of a chat show announcing the next act.

'Do you know who he is?' she would say before launching into a great sales pitch, emphasising the virtues of donating to my cause, Newman School.

I would more often than not come away with a few bob stuffed into my camelback; I much preferred notes, of course, as coins were much too heavy to carry over any distance…

After leaving Diane I set off running down the towpath towards Worksop – the furthest point of that day's marathon – before heading back across the fields to the outskirts of Langold, through Firbeck village and then home to Maltby.

This cross-country route saw me completing just under twenty-seven miles during this, the seventeenth marathon.

Before finally reaching home every day I would call into Maltby Service Station, just a few hundred yards from my home, to have my daily Garmin watch results logged, verified witnessed and adjudicated by the Mellor family who ran the garage.

My Garmin watch, which I used every day, displays the distance covered and time it took, while I would provide the rough location of each daily marathon.

Dave and his sons, Mike and Neil, had agreed some time ago to provide support and be witnesses to the daily marathons by routinely logging all the details onto a file of seventy-five sheets, which had been designed and produced by Dave's wife, Eileen.

I would hand over my watch, usually before 4:30pm, to any one of the guys who would then record the day's marathon information onto the allocated spreadsheet. After signing the sheet, they'd then remove the day's data from my Garmin watch, leaving me with a clean blank screen in readiness for the following day. This simple recording system provided an accurate account of each day's marathon, adding adjudicated credibility to my challenge.

A great, simple system which worked well.

I take great pleasure reliving these marathons when reading through these statistical sheets, whenever I am in need of a bit of inspiration.

Having spent many hours on my computer prior to the start date mapping out various accurate twenty-six-plus mile routes on Google Maps in and around Rotherham, Worksop, Sheffield and Doncaster, it was reassuring that the daily results on my Garmin provided almost the same mileage.

I never actually managed to run the exact 26.2 miles. Always over and sometimes over twenty-eight miles. But then what's a couple of miles between friends?

Rony Robinson wasn't the only media personality interested in my challenge. The boost this fundraising event needed arrived just prior to getting the challenge underway with a surprise phone call from the BBC.

A week or so before the start date, I was leaving I-Motion gym after final arrangements had been made to sort out the logos for the marathon T-shirts. Whilst I was about to start my car, I received a phone call showing an unrecognised number.

'Hello, Ray, it's Nicola.'

'Sorry,' I said. 'Nicola who?'

'It's Nicola Rees from BBC Look North.'

Bloody hell. Shock, and I think I was even blushing!

As we exchanged pleasantries, I started to recognise her voice from the frequent interviews I had seen of her on TV.

'Ray, I hear that you're about to run seventy-five consecutive marathons starting on your seventy-fifth birthday, is that right?'

She listened intently while I confirmed that's just what I would be setting out to do, and then convincingly assuring her I would manage this challenge.

'Can I come over and do an interview?' she asked, after she became confident that this was not some April Fools' hoax. 'Let me have your address and I will come over to you. Is there somewhere close by where we could do some filming?' she asked.

'Take your pick, we have loads of great sites around to do some filming. Roche Abbey would be a great visual location if you fancy that,' I ventured.

We agreed a time of around 10:30am for the following morning. I was excited to be getting some TV coverage to help kick-start the fundraising, and this would be a very first for me.

But how very naive of me, as I later mulled over the thought of being part of a televised news show. I envisaged great problems arising with the BBC trying to get one of those whacking great big broadcast trucks, you know, the ones with the big dishes on top, down the very narrow lane, ripping out all the overhead phone lines on the way down to our cottage.

I needn't have worried. Nicola turned up in her little Mini

the following morning and produced a pretty smart, state-of-the-art handheld camera.

After a few minutes of introductions and ideas about what Nicola wanted for the six o'clock evening news filming, I suggested we head down to the historic Roche Abbey, a couple of miles away, pointing to the path through the lichen gate of St Bartholomew's church.

Not only is this former monastery one of Rotherham's finest heritage landmarks, but it's also surrounded by plenty of great countryside and even a picturesque waterfall at the north-eastern end of the lake that would provide a great backdrop for any filming.

Check me out. I was beginning to sound like a regular pro who did this sort of thing every day.

But there would be no running down the path to the Abbey.

'Can we get there by car?' was Nicola's next question.

After driving down the two and a half mile by-road, we entered the Abbey grounds by driving down the old, cobbled stone road to the car park below.

We parked and set off out around the quiet paths close to the Abbey to identify ideal spots to film me running and conduct the interviews.

The trails across and alongside the waterfall were perfect for what she wanted and the light was adequate for the direction of my running! Hell's bells, it seemed like we were about to make a blockbuster movie. Nicola even had me running with her phone on the end of one of those new-fangled selfie sticks.

Nicola, I soon realised, was a perfectionist. Everything had to be spot on, even to the extent of her completely deleting a good session purely because of a light noise from a passing plane on its way to some faraway place from Doncaster Sheffield Airport.

She is a runner herself and accompanied me on some of the footage during the 'on the run' interviews.

'I know you don't want a lot of fuss, Ray, but I have bought you a birthday cake,' she casually mentioned as we approached her car, me thinking we had finished my very first TV interview. 'I have an idea,' she said, asking me if I knew where we could place the cake.

I suggested the large wooden gate post at the entry to the Abbey, once she had explained what she had in mind.

Nicola placed the cake, about a foot in diameter with frilly wrapping around the middle, on top of the wooden post and strategically set the camera up behind so it would capture us both running towards it.

She lit the number seven and five candles and switched on the camera; the cake wasn't big enough to accommodate seventy-five individual candles!

Her idea was that we run up to the cake from the Abbey, I was to look surprised as we approached the cake, Nicola would then say, 'Happy birthday, Ray, now make a wish,' and after my comment, I'd blow out the candles. Job done. Interview over.

OK, that shouldn't be too difficult, I thought. Should it?

We set off running back from the Abbey towards the cake and awaiting camera, but less than ten feet from our destination the candles blew out.

Nicola lit the candles again; we retraced our steps down to the Abbey some hundred yards away and set off again at an even faster pace this time towards our target.

The candles had extinguished themselves again, this time as we arrived at the cake.

Take three – candles still not playing ball.

Takes four, five and six – candles seemed to have a mind of their own and not playing the game with us, but Nicola was determined to get this part of the filming done, on script!

It really didn't seem that windy to me – perhaps one of the Cistercian Monk ghosts was playing a trick on us.

And then on take seven, as we were approaching the cake, using the now well-worn path, Nicola said, 'Ray, don't forget to look surprised.'

I couldn't suppress the chuckling and then, between fits of laughter, said, 'I am totally surprised, Nicola; I'm surprised nobody has nicked the bloody cake while we have been running up and down.'

That very first filming episode felt like completing a marathon! But perfection comes at a cost, and the end results of it showed on the final version which was aired just after 6:45pm on the BBC Look North news programme. I wasn't at all surprised to see that the funny part of the filming had been edited out.

That evening my phone never stopped ringing with excited friends informing me that I was, or had been, 'on't telly'.

It's a strange sensation watching yourself on terrestrial TV for the very first time.

Nicola has kept in touch and, from time to time, provided further coverage which always made a massive difference to the fundraising total, especially the days after the programme had been shown.

The *big* day – launch day – finally arrived and as I made

my way down to Herringthorpe Stadium on the outskirts of Rotherham to start the first marathon on Saturday 2nd July, I was finding it hard to suppress the excitement that was running through my body.

Both BBC and ITV camera crews were inside the stadium waiting for me to arrive. I was amazed at the number of people who were also there waiting, many of whom had come down to run the first mile with me on the track.

Holly, my beautiful granddaughter who had been at the start of all my previous challenges, was there, all bright and cheerful, waiting for me like a good-luck charm. How could I ever doubt that I would be successful with her by my side?

The Rotherham Advertiser coverage over the weeks leading up to that day had had a huge impact, providing great exposure and information about the challenge which was now just an hour away from getting started.

It was heart-warming to see so many people of Rotherham out in force at the stadium, both as spectators and participants, to witness and run the first mile with me at the start of the seventy-five marathons.

Sean had set up the morning's interview timings with both TV reporters and press. All I had to do was just turn up, look pretty and answer a few choice questions.

When I look back at photos and video footage from that very first film interview with ITV, looking every bit the part of a professional athlete, in a smart green Hummel-sponsored tracksuit, I have to chuckle as it looked as though I had been doing these sorts of things forever. I was leant on the rails above the track looking nonchalant, full of confidence, and relaxed, as if it's something I did every day.

To tell the truth, I was petrified and full of trepidation,

but working very hard to keep it together and not show how much I was shaking.

It's a self-inflicted challenge, anyway, so why was I putting myself through this thing?!

'I'll be OK once I get going,' I kept saying to that little imp whom I had managed over the years to control but who was once again sat on my shoulder.

This event had now gone far beyond being only about my personal challenge with the need to satisfy just me. There was much, much more at stake now and the need to pull off this, the most extreme of all challenges. It had become more important than anything I had ever done before.

'*I can do this.*'

The big black BMW 7 series mayoral car had arrived at the stadium and the occupants who had alighted stood patiently waiting for my interviews to finish.

The Rotherham mayor, Lyndsay Pitchley, had been unavailable, but our more than willing deputy mayor had agreed to attend and start my challenge off today.

Cllr Eve Rose Keenan stepped out of the car and entered Herringthorpe Stadium, the home of Rotherham Harriers, dressed in a colourful flowery dress with a small gold medallion pinned to her.

Once I realised she was wearing running shoes, I guessed that she would be running the first mile as well, so it made good sense why she was without mayoral chains. Much easier to control the three-inch medallion than the huge gold civic regalia she would normally wear.

Eve and her six-foot-odd-tall husband, Pat, were introduced to me by her also not-so-little official driver, Dean Walton.

It was hard to get my head around the image in front of me because I could never have imagined that a real-life deputy mayor would be taking any physical part in my challenge.

Eve soon put me at ease, instantly doing away with any formal protocol in a flash – a real down-to-earth, easy-to-get-on-with character. We became instant friends and have supported one another over the years.

Press interviews concluded, followed by photo shoots with Dave Poucher from the *Rotherham Advertiser*, and then it was down onto the red oval running track and start line with my friends, running buddies, some of the children from Newman School and our deputy mayor partly dressed in running gear.

We all lined up behind the white marked-out start line, trying desperately to keep the young children in check. After a short speech from me, thanking everyone for their attendance, we began the countdown which was loudly shouted out with enthusiasm, especially from the young children.

Ten, nine, eight, seven, six, we chanted. Even louder came five, four, three, two, one. Time to get this challenge started. *Go!*

My heart nearly bounced out of my chest with that great, proud feeling that can only come from this sort of occasion. And we're off.

The first marathon got underway, well, more like a stampede from the kids, I suppose, as we all headed for Dave Poucher, who was positioned about fifty yards in the middle of the home straight of the running track, camera clicking away, working overtime to capture memories for the future.

Both BBC and ITV were strategically placed at the track side, also capturing this exciting moment in time which was aired on both channels later during the evening news programmes.

Most of the kids had passed me well before the hundred-metre mark.

What a fantastic sight of colourful clad athletes, children in school colours waving flags, wheelchairs with brightly coloured wheel discs and parents in their casual gear, all determined to complete that first mile with me.

One of the most humbling experiences and proudest moments in my life.

How high is it possible to get, legally, without floating off into space?

I was feeling on top of the world, bursting at the seams with contentment after completing the four laps of the track with everyone.

It was now time to leave the track and, after saying my thanks and goodbyes to everyone, I ran out of the stadium and headed for the streets to run the bulk of the 26.2 miles around the circumference of Herringthorpe.

Lap after lap of street running finally provided the distance I needed to eventually leave the roads and head towards Clifton Park. But during the first twenty-four miles or so, I experienced nearly all four seasons of weather in one day: sun mid-morning, through driving rain to freezing cold. It was so cold that Dominic Hurley, wearing lightweight clothing and cycling at a relatively slow pace to accompany me, had to be ordered home to warm up!

During the last lap, I was accompanied by a rejuvenated Dominic on his bike and friend and running colleague, Phil

Harris, who joined me as I once again passed the stadium for the last time. Phil is also a representative of GMB Union, who had not only sponsored this first marathon but, very generously, the seventy-fifth as well.

As I checked my Garmin watch in anticipation, now heading for Clifton Park, I was pleased to see that I had reached my goal of a little over the 26.2 miles just before we entered the Clifton Lane entrance into the park.

Job done. I had more than completed the first marathon distance already. Satisfied, I looked forward to meeting my wife Maureen in just a couple of minutes.

Feeling a bit leggy, but more than pleased to be still running strongly, we headed into Clifton Park, taking the tree-lined middle path down the hill towards the bandstand where a large crowd were waiting to greet me.

The avenue of banners in the distance which narrowed down to the bandstand were soon visible. I spotted Maureen, who had been sat patiently waiting on the bandstand steps with Mary and Ken Chapman, in among the many friends who had come to see me through the finish line of this inaugural marathon. I could hear the cheering as we approached the bandstand and the last couple of yards of this the first of seventy-five marathons.

A bite to eat and a bottle of Lucozade was followed by a short speech from a very enthusiastic Eric Batty, the late GMB Rotherham branch secretary who sadly passed away in January 2019. It was then time to head home and prepare for the second sponsored marathon.

I was booked to run the Brinsworth 10K with many of my friends and local club runners early next morning.

There were many important elements and factors coming

together that made this challenge less of a risk than most people thought possible. Nutrition was one and played an important part during these marathons.

Team member Barry Close, friend and long-standing club colleague, had talked endlessly about his concern of potential severe muscle damage through dehydration and lack of body fat which could greatly compound over a short space of time during the early marathons.

Progressive weight loss could render me incapable of completing the challenge long before the seventy-fifth, as Barry had explained during our team talks. Just the loss of half a per cent of bodyweight each day would quickly equate to a staggering twenty-five per cent of deterioration, leading to serious problems and the probability that medical treatment would be needed, rendering the challenge dangerously beyond our control.

Having listened to his concerns, it made perfect sense to address this possible lethal problem. After all, this sort of extended challenge was new to me.

Now, I am no specialist on this subject, but as I understand it in simple terms, the food we eat, and in particular carbohydrates, which are basically simple sugars, are stored in the muscles as glycogen.

When we begin to exercise, our muscles release the glycogen in the form of energy to drive our muscles. When energy levels dwindle your body releases fatty acids (fat) into your bloodstream, which looks for even more carbs from the food we have eaten to refuel the muscles. If we are not eating enough carbs then the fatty acids can't convert to glycogen and hence fully refuel the muscles.

Worse still, the body will seek out an alternative fuel –

protein. If you're not eating enough protein the body will start to cannibalise muscles and prevent them from repairing after exercise or, in my case, during a long-distance run.

When you run again you start with a slightly lower tank each time. Your body will keep releasing fats so you lose even more weight, but more importantly you are losing muscle mass, which is far denser, so you start to lose weight even quicker.

You then have a combination of fat loss, muscle loss, low energy conversion and lack of muscle repair. Next step, hospital on a drip like Eddie Izzard during his twenty-seven marathons in South Africa!

An analogy is like when your drive a car you start with a full tank. Each day you drive it and don't fill up the tank, inevitably eventually the car will come to a complete stop.

This is not an attempt to sensationalise the importance of correct fuelling to be able to take on and perform feats of endurance, but merely to enlighten you, the reader.

Greater detail is contained in Barry's guest contribution at the end of this chapter.

Barry's concern stemmed from and was highlighted by Eddie Izzard's attempt to run twenty-seven consecutive marathons in South Africa – the 'Nelson Mandela Marathons' – in February 2016 just four months before my own challenge.

A self-confessed non-runner, Eddie, at the age of fifty-four, had bravely decided to run a marathon for every year of Nelson Mandela's twenty-seven years of incarceration, covering 707.4 miles, often in extreme heat.

But the real issue for me came during day five of Eddie's challenge when, following medical advice due to heat exhaustion, dehydration and who knows what else, he was rushed to a local hospital and placed on a drip to aid recovery.

The success of the hospitalisation enabled him to continue and courageously complete his challenge. Eddie managed to complete two marathons during the last day to make up for the loss of the sixth day spent recovering in hospital.

I remember feeling a real concern for him while watching film coverage of him in bed with the drip attached to his arm in some South African hospital.

To be brutally honest, I hadn't given nutritional supplement much thought up to this point, mainly because although I had lost the best part of a stone in weight during the recent Sahara Desert race, I usually peak and level off at my fighting weight of around ten stone. A perfect weight that works for me. That said, I had never attempted a challenge that took multiple weeks to complete. Better to be safe than sorry and risk failing in my attempt through lack of nutrition.

With the help of one of my sponsors, Rick Thompson, the new owner of I-Motion gym, Barry and I were provided with a contact who Rick thought would be able to help provide the nutritional supplement I would need.

Three weeks before the challenge started, we made contact with Body Building Warehouse, a leading American supplement company, and, after a short telephone conversation, arranged for Barry and me to visit their warehouse on the outskirts of Manchester.

They were fascinated with my challenge as we discussed my needs. Their initial response was that my challenge was miles away from what they specialised in. However, after a meaningful conversation with their in-house specialist scientists and chemists, dressed in immaculate white laboratory gowns, Barry and the company manager came up with a solution they were happy to support.

My need for a slow-release energy supplement, totally opposite to the normal quick energy-giving supplement Body Building Warehouse are renowned for, provided something of a challenge for them. But, after further discussions, a couple of products were identified as a perfect solution by using a mixture of carbs and protein that would have the desired effect we were after.

Barry negotiated and agreed upon a two- to three-week regular supply of the mix we needed and which they were happy to supply.

We came away with hundreds of pounds' worth of best-quality carbs and protein, together with a few boxes of their latest protein energy bars.

New to this supplement game, I had no idea that the overall cost of keeping my weight in check could have been so costly, if I had had to pay.

Barry had also worked out and provided a chart that would provide me with an additional intake of at least 2,500 calories a day. Most of these were to be consumed during breakfast, which consisted of four Weetabix, around half a pint of full-fat milk, sweetened by a large spoonful of honey and topped with half a banana. Not done there: two slices of toast, swimming in Lurpak butter and honey, were followed by a glass full of the remainder of the pint of full-fat milk mixed with the carbs and protein supplement.

Imagine running with that lot inside you?

It did become easier after only a few days into the marathons and became part of my daily routine, which I followed religiously.

An evening weigh-in and another as I got out of bed the following morning closely monitored my daily weight. The results were registered on a chart and relayed back to Barry for analysis, followed by any adjustment ratio between carbs and protein to keep my weight at a constant ten stone.

My weight did drop during the first two weeks from ten and a half stone down to ten stone dead, as I had predicted. After all, this is my optimum "fighting weight", which, during the first few marathons, became a bit of concern for Barry. After this, my weight levelled out and only fluctuated an ounce or so around ten stone for the remainder of the marathons.

A huge weight-management success, I must admit, and a massive thanks to Barry and to Body Building Warehouse.

Throughout the seventy-five marathons, I consumed around 40kg of carbs, 20kg of protein and around fourteen boxes of protein bars!

*

Guest Contribution

Barry Close

I am indebted to Barry for all that he did before and during the challenge. He has a wealth of knowledge about nutrition which was key in me being able to complete my challenge.

Ray Matthews

I first became aware of Ray about ten years ago when I was on a trip to Prague with my partner, Claire.

It was a warm, sunny day so we took a walk along the riverside. As we came down the hill towards the river it was obvious something was happening. I could see the traffic being held back and there were lots of people in yellow vests dotted around.

As we got closer, I saw runners crossing the bridge; I'd seen a poster advertising the Prague Marathon, so it wasn't rocket science to work out this was the day.

We stood and watched the runners when suddenly Claire said, 'He goes to our gym!,' pointing to a man who had just passed in front of us. I wasn't sure, but she was convinced she had seen him in the gym.

I didn't give it much thought until a few weeks later, after training one morning, a few of us were having a coffee and putting the world to rights. Someone sat behind me mentioned Prague and I turned to see Ray. He said he had recently taken part in the marathon there, to which I added, 'He did, I saw him.'

As we spoke over the next few months and years whenever we met in the gym, I found out more about Ray's accomplishments.

Soon the conversations turned to how Ray was planning to celebrate his seventy-fifth birthday. He had the idea of running seventy-five marathons in seventy-five consecutive days. Impossible for anyone, I thought, never mind a seventy-five-year-old man!

But Ray really wanted to do this. More importantly, he was confident he could achieve it. If he had the right help.

I started to investigate the logistics a little deeper: where he would run, how he could bring in sponsors to raise funds for his chosen charity.

The more I thought about it, and the more people I spoke to in the trade, the more I realised just what a monumental challenge this was for anyone, never mind a man of Ray's years. My forty-odd years in the gym told me his muscles would be in tatters after a week or so as they struggled to recover from such a punishing schedule.

My contribution would be to help him curtail this damage through nutrition, which was daunting in itself. It wasn't simply a matter of cramming him full of food and hoping for the best; we needed to control the effect such a punishing schedule would have on his whole-body composition.

How would Ray minimise the inevitable weight loss and muscle damage and the less evident, but equally important, psychological effects that such a lengthy challenge would certainly bring?

Six months before Ray started his marathons, I contacted some of the better-known supplement companies to discuss possible sponsorship, hoping they would lend their sports scientists and professional nutritionists to offer advice, and of course their products. Nobody took us seriously as, one after the other, they declined.

Ironically, it was a casual chat with Rick, one of the owners at I-Motion gym, that started the ball rolling.

They'd already provided shirt sponsorship, but more importantly they introduced me to their sports supplement supplier, Body Building Warehouse, a 'new kid on the block' at the time that was building a reputation for cutting-edge nutrition products.

Ray and I were invited to the warehouse in Manchester to discuss the project and our requirements with the owner. They agreed to supply Ray with 5kg tubs of whey protein, huge bags of weight-gain powders, maltodextrin (carbs) and box after box of their protein bars for him to snack on as he ran. If we needed more, they said just ask and they'd drop it off.

The next task was to get back in the gym to try and determine the calories Ray would burn off during his run. We didn't have access to the state-of-the-art machines and professional software, but we did it the best we could with the gym's treadmills. Ray ran at a steady 8K for sixty minutes, a pace he said he could do all day, and then I used the treadmill's computer to calculate calories burned based on his age and weight, etc. It wasn't precise but was a good guide to calculate an approximate figure from which I could work out the nutrition required to maintain his current bodyweight as much as possible.

The next step was to analyse Ray's diet to determine how he was going to add the additional 2,500+ calories per day required. Ray completed a seven-day food diary, logging everything he ate and drank, so I could work out his normal calorie intake. We soon realised that, on top of his normal meals, he was going to need a large amount of supplements to keep things moving.

Timing was key. It would be challenging to get these extra calories into his body during the eight hours or so when Ray wasn't either running or sleeping, without leaving him feeling bloated.

As Ray stepped up the training in the weeks leading up to the start date, he started adding supplements into his daily diet then we refined it until we found what was considered the right balance for him.

Once the challenge started, Ray needed to weigh himself each morning before he ran and then again in the evening when he returned. Initially, Ray felt he needed to drop three or four kilos to achieve his optimum running weight. To achieve this, we adjusted his supplement intake to allow a gradual drop in bodyweight, while also making sure he still had sufficient nutrition to repair and refuel to complete the following day's run.

After a few days, Ray reached his ideal weight. Then it was a case of trying to maintain it over the next seventy-odd marathons.

Each day Ray filled in a form we had devised which included his pre- and post-run bodyweight, the duration of the run and a star rating system to indicate how he felt both mentally and physically prior to and after the run – one being poor and five being excellent.

It wasn't a totally scientific exercise. We were very much flying by wires, making adjustments each day or, to be more precise, every other day as we found there was lag between each change. For example, as his carbohydrate intake increased, the results became noticeable to Ray the day after.

On the whole, Ray managed to maintain his weight to within one kilo, thanks in part to keeping fuelled all times.

About seven or eight marathons into the challenge, Ray started to feel tight in his glutes and hamstrings; this was normal, if you can call running a marathon every day for a week normal! His body was struggling to repair itself in the short rest period between the runs. To maximise his muscle repair, we began constantly monitoring his protein/carb ratios.

While the challenge was taking its toll on his legs, as Ray got into the last dozen or so marathons, he said he still felt fresh.

He made it, though, and achieved his goal. Ray did all the hard work; I just added in a little knowledge along the way.

5

From school to Steelos

I left school in the summer of 1956 and leapt, with eyes wide open, into a new way of life as a wage-earner. There hadn't been much of a ceremony at St Bede's, not that I expected one! However, during that last day, Mr Flynn summoned me out to the front with his right arm around my shoulder and announced, to the whole class, that I was destined to do great things. I have often reflected on that comment over the years, but in all honesty I think most of the teaching staff were glad to see the back of me.

Part of evolution, after leaving school it was expected of me to find a job and become a wage-earning contributor to the Matthews household. Options were extremely limited for a fifteen-year-old without academic qualifications.

Take your pick: steelworks or mining were the most viable and readily available choices on the table in and around an industrial town like Rotherham.

It had almost been inevitable that I would be offered a job

at Steelos. I didn't even have to be interviewed; my passport to employment was already stamped via my boxing for the company. The job was mine, I was told some months before leaving school, if I wanted it…

Within two weeks of leaving school, I was heading out across Masbrough to the steelworks between Ickles and Templeborough. I was about to be inducted into a new way of life at the largest steel manufacturing company in South Yorkshire, Steel, Peech and Tozer, who at that time employed over eleven thousand in their workforce, and now me!

It was a Monday in early August and I was on my way to work, running like hell for the three and a half miles from my home, with a haversack full of sandwiches, to make the 8am clocking-in time at the Rotherham Melting Shop metallurgy offices.

With a wage of three pounds and eight shilling a week, I was now a major contributor to our family income, slightly easing the daily poverty we had experienced for most of my young life.

Steel, Peech and Tozer, one of Rotherham's largest employers, ran a scheme which helped introduce young employees to the extreme dangers attached to the enormous steel manufacturing plant.

Newly recruited fifteen-year-olds were stationed in offices around various sections of the plant to acclimatise for the first twelve months, before settling into full-time permanent jobs.

Together with a group of about fifteen other school leavers, I had attended an induction course the previous week and had been supplied, from the works' stores, with my first pair of black steel toe-capped leather boots that I would pay for out of my weekly wage.

After a short film about our new working environment,

we were told of our roles and where we would be stationed for a four-month period, until advised of our next move to some other location around the plant.

It was dangerous, noisy and hot. The filthy dust billowing out of the chimneys of the blast furnaces was a normal day-to-day sight, covering everything that didn't move in thick, red dust. The noise and steel sparks flying all over the place, illuminating the furnace platform, was frightening at first but soon became second nature.

These conditions were readily accepted by everyone at that time, just part of the steel-manufacturing process, and who was I to complain?

Once I had settled in and found my way around the melting shop and surrounding areas, nobody seemed to be bothered about me as long as I was around on time to pick up metal samples from the white-hot molten mix.

Then, after metallurgical analysis had taken place, I would take the results back to the head furnaceman for modifications to the mix. I had loads of free time in between casts. A doddle of a job.

It took me just a couple of weeks to realise I could make some serious extra money when I found out that returning an empty third of a pint milk bottle to the canteen was worth a penny.

There were hundreds of these little glass bottles just lying about gathering dust under the soakers and furnace staging that had been discarded by the furnacemen and kiln workers. Throughout each shift, they consumed copious amounts of milk, as it settled the lungs, apparently.

Who in their right mind would bother walking all the way to the canteen to return an empty bottle for a penny?

It didn't take long for me to establish a great little business collecting and recycling these small milk bottles. To add to the weekly turnover, I ensured possession of each empty bottle by collecting milk from the canteen and delivering it to the thirsty workers. In no time at all I had a better milk round than our milkman at home! Soon I was making more on my milk round than my wages – and tax-free! But don't say owt.

My first wage packet and pay slip revealed that all eleven thousand-plus workers voluntarily paid one penny each week into the social services fund which was used to supplement all the sporting amenities and activities that Steel, Peech and Tozer provided for its employees. I was now contributing to my own benefits that I had so gratefully been receiving over the years through boxing.

I remember some weeks after my induction, during a conversation I had with Jacky Pearson at training one evening, mentioning my concern about how the steelworks' dusty environment would affect my health, and thus my sporting ability over time. I didn't really expect that my comments would influence any change; after all, I was now working alongside these tough steelworkers. But change did happen.

A couple of weeks later a letter attached to my clock card revealed that I was instructed to attend a meeting in the social service office later that day.

'Ray, in view of your boxing and sporting commitment to our company, I have secured a position for you at the Phoenix Golf Course. Would you please report to the head groundsman Monday morning at eight o'clock sharp?'

Although I couldn't remember the name of the man I was

talking to, he looked familiar. I had seen him at the gym on occasions handing over what looked like a small pay packet to Jacky Pearson.

I would have to forfeit my very lucrative milk round – hope the new boy would have the sense to figure it out – but £3–8s a week for working out in the sun, away from all that dust and grime, sounded great to me.

I would be working in the fresh air, which was certainly a much healthier proposition for me. As long as the wind wasn't blowing in the wrong direction, bringing that red dust up from the melting shops and rolling mills over the hill to settle on the eighteen-hole golf course in Brinsworth, I would be fine!

As luck would have it, we experienced an extended fabulous summer that year, with me working the eight-hour day shift in just a pair of shorts, month after month. What more could a young man want? I was being paid to keep fit.

I fitted in nicely with my new job, picking up what was expected of me in no time, although I felt that the head groundsman didn't seem to want me around. At the start of each day, I was given work, most of which was out on the course and miles away from the clubhouse, and told to get on with it. There was always plenty to keep me busy with.

I quickly learned that one of his big "Do Not Touch" areas centred around the greens, which were his pride and joy, and lovingly received his daily attention, especially the eighteenth in front of the clubhouse that looked immaculate.

Whilst scything long grass (there was plenty of that), I soon realised that many a lost golf ball was hiding just waiting for me to find. Before long, I had a large bag of balls that I had collected, which came in handy as I had started playing during lunchtime, using the newly acquired golf clubs that I had also found out on the course!

An idea clicked into place during a conversation I had had with one of the golfers whilst scything down some long grass on the edge of the course. He offered to give me tuppence for any balls I found that were decent and not badly damaged. But even better still, threepence for any Titleist or Slazenger balls, if I could find them.

Just a quick wash down in the groundsman's cabin enhanced the look of the balls, making them even more presentable and saleable. It didn't take long for word to get round the golfers that I was selling second-hand balls. Soon, I was earning more from the sale of golf balls than my wages!

The head groundsman wanted a cut once he found out what I was up to. 'Anything you find on the golf course belongs to me,' he said, the robbing dog!

The exploitation didn't last long, though, after I caught him in a very compromising position with a young woman one afternoon. She was bent over the work bench close to the fire with her knickers around her ankles and the rest of her clothes on the bench at the back of our cabin (of course I looked!). He suddenly forgot to ask for his weekly cut after that!

The sights that I saw on that golf course over the summer, if I worked quietly, ha-ha. Believe me, I could write a book…

I loved this great new way of life of working, training and fighting. I was fit, by God I was fit. It was impossible to just walk; I almost always ran everywhere. Even getting to work every day, I would run from my home in Masbrough, down the old narrow cinder track alongside the southern turnstiles of Rotherham United's Millmoor football stadium.

The Path to Success

The football ground and surrounding area at that time was owned by the chairman Ken Booth, who also owned a large scrap business that ran alongside and behind the stadium. The pitch itself was overlooked by the large overhead crane towering high above the scrap yard alongside the west stand.

Some years earlier, I frequented this ground as the Rotherham United mascot. Every Saturday's home game I would be picked up from my home in Holland Place by a couple of the players: Nobby Noble, who lived just round the corner on Brown Street, and goalkeeper Jock Quairny, who lived just below us on Holland Street. We would walk up to the stadium with the rest of the crowd. Great memories.

*

My fight record was now becoming a bit of a cross to bear, I reckoned, making it difficult to find local opponents to match against. From regularly fighting weekly, I was now lucky to get a fight once a month. But the opponents I did get were much more talented and increasingly more difficult to fight against. I had to be on my A-game all the time and the distance I had to travel to get matched up also added to the frustration.

Not yet a senior, I had on occasions agreed to fight against seventeen- and eighteen-year-old opponents, often giving away pounds in weight.

One evening, Jacky and Jack Cox were waiting for me as I walked through the big brown doors into the gym, beckoning me over and waving a letter in the air that had arrived from the well-known boxing promoter Jack Solomons.

I was unaware, at the time, who Jack Solomons was and how influential and important this man had become in the professional British boxing world. On a similar par to Eddie Hearn today, I would say.

'Ray, we are being asked to make a comment about your future and your prospects about turning professional. He wants to sign you up. This is so exciting for you,' Jack Cox said with genuine delight. They were both more excited than I was. An enquiry from Jack Solomons was not an everyday occurrence and definitely a first for our club, I was told.

Even though I had given it some thought of late, technically I couldn't even apply for a licence to become a professional boxer until I was eighteen and that was still more than a couple of years away. But because I'd already been fighting seventeen- and eighteen-year-olds, the assumption was made that I'd be ready for the next step.

This was not the last I heard from Mr Solomons, who kept in touch by letter a couple of times a year.

I had many sleepless nights thinking about this huge next step in my career, a decision I feared I would have to make sooner rather than later.

Torn between my love of boxing and the commitment to financially helping at home, I knew it wouldn't be long before I would have to choose. But whilst weighing up all the pros and cons of turning professional, I always seemed to come to the same conclusion.

By then, as a sixteen-year-old, having served my time out on the golf course, I had secured a job in the highest-paid rolling mill in the company. I was now working in the cogging mill, on a three-shift continental rota system, taking home a huge pay packet and heavily contributing to our family coffers.

Yet, on the other hand, new professional boxers at my

weight were lucky to make £25 a fight, which would be depleted rapidly by having to pay trainers, seconds and all other expenses out of the fight purse. I was earning almost that amount each week now. It seemed a no-brainer to me.

How ironic is it that, as I sit here today and write about my life at that time facing a decision that would determine my future, I reflect on the massive difference today's young fighters are faced with. Now, after only a handful of professional fights, they are matched up and fighting for European and World titles, being paid huge sums of money, often reaching hundreds of thousands of pounds.

It makes me cringe when I read about this "status quo" because for everyone who makes it, I fear there are thousands who don't. Nobody should ever be put on that merry-go-round, like lumps of meat in the slaughterhouse, without the years of learning their trade.

Ever think you were born in the wrong era? Anyway, rant over!

I was still enjoying my fighting and the new experience of mixing work with boxing. The elite privileges I was being afforded at this time in my boxing career certainly made life much easier than it would have been working for any other company.

Shift working could have made life difficult, but I was given hours, even days, off with pay to fight, or even attend the gym for training leading up to important fights. I wanted for nothing: the best kit, the best transport to and from events, the best hotels, and now shifts and days off with pay. Even professional fighters couldn't better that, I reckoned.

I hadn't had a local fight for well over twelve months, which meant that I had become used to travelling the length and breadth of England, where I wasn't as well known, to get matched up. London gyms were fairly regular providers of fight opponents, along with Liverpool, Cardiff and Newcastle, which meant hotel stays or long hours of travelling, with even the odd time on my own, too.

At last, a request to fight came in at a midweek evening amateur boxing event somewhere on the outskirts of Cardiff. I was being matched up with a Welsh National Coal Board champion who, as had become the norm with my opponents at that time, possessed an impressive fight record.

A year older than me, and I suspect a few pounds heavier, we stood facing one another in the ring. I had missed the weigh-in because the train was late for some reason or other, which resulted in missing our bus connection to the fight venue, making it a rush to get ready for the fight on time.

When my opponent and I came together for the first time, we were in this ring being introduced to the boisterous crowd in this smoke-filled hall who were roaring with excitement in the build-up to our bout.

It was always a thrilling experience to be part of that razzamatazz build-up that I have only ever encountered with boxing, especially when you hear your name being announced to the crowd by an over-exaggerated compere.

'And in the red corner, representing the Phoenix Boxing Club. All the way from Sheffield, Yorkshire.'

Why do they always say Sheffield? 'I am from Rotherham,' I wanted to shout.

'Raaaaaaay Matthews.'

Which was greeted with a modicum of cheers mixed with a share of booing. I loved it when the crowd got involved, either for or against.

I had travelled down on the train from Sheffield with Jimmy, our usual second-in-command and regular cornerman. Unfortunately, Jacky Pearson couldn't make it due to a prior commitment.

My opponent, a good few inches taller, towered over me as we came together to receive our pre-fight instructions from the immaculately dressed referee. Snow-white shirt with black dicky-bow, black slacks with creases that would fetch blood if touched and black shoes with a shine you could see your face in.

His pre-rehearsed instructions delivered like a well-orchestrated recording.

'In the event of a knock-down, you must go to a neutral corner. No hitting below the belt. You must obey my instructions at all times and defend yourself at all times. Good luck,' followed by arms pointing in different directions indicating return to your corners.

Jimmy checked my gloves over, making sure that both white laces were tucked in, offered up my moist gum shield and patted my back. 'Go get him,' he said.

The bell sounded for the opening round and we inched our way together in the middle of the ring like gladiators eyeing one another up, ready to do battle.

From past experiences, it was always my aim to dominate and fight from the centre of the ring, making my opponent use up energy as they were made to circle in a wider arc.

But what I wasn't ready for was the boxing talent that my opponent possessed; the speed of his jabs and footwork were frustratingly awesome. And as he was quite clearly taller than me, he created an instant gap between us. He was in and out like lightning.

The length of his arms and speed of his footwork meant that he was able to keep me far enough away from him, to stop me getting near enough to connect with any punches and prevent me from scoring.

That first round at the Red Lion boxing club with Cloggy Clarke came swiftly to mind. This guy was fast and also, like Cloggy, seemed to possess more arms than me. I was being out-boxed.

My analysis of the fight mid-round was that, even though I was proficiently blocking most of his punches and ducking under his crosses, it certainly didn't equate to points scored, which actually meant I was not winning this fight; he was. This was definitely not part of the script.

I wasn't getting hurt, but I was also not stopping all his jabs getting through. Hell's bells! He was fast and it was me who was back-pedalling and using up much energy trying to avoid getting a proper pasting.

Round one ended with me on the receiving end of some lightning-quick jabs. Fortunately for me, the power didn't match his speed. I wasn't in any danger of being physically hurt, but my pride was taking an all-mighty battering.

I didn't need to sit during the one-minute break, and just stood facing Jimmy as he sponged me down.

'Ray you're gonna have to fight this one. Forget about boxing. Get inside and make it count. Let's see how he copes with some good body shots.'

Wise words from Jimmy, and something that I should have been able to analyse for myself before the end of that first round.

That's all it needed: Jimmy stating the obvious. A solution is always there if you look for it.

The bell sounded for round two and there was a similar start, but this time I was on a mission, reverting back to my scrapping days.

Time to become a fighter again had been my thoughts and new strategy during the interval.

It soon became crystal-clear that if I could stay close to him, he would be unable to punch from long arms that were being tied up.

I could hear the frantic cries from his trainer to get away from me as I backed him into his corner. The ring was closing in on my opponent as I hounded him, using pure reaction speed to stay close and deliver heavy telling body hooks.

He didn't like being hit in the stomach, and a couple of times he doubled up as the hooks connected. I kept up this barrage of heavy body shots ducking under any attempt of retaliation from him.

This new tactic was working and giving me targets that were not available during the first round.

But that's easier said than done, my friend, because it meant a non-stop attack with both hands, relying on my super fitness, reaction speed and not allowing him to settle into his way of boxing.

Trying to get away from the onslaught I was now dishing out, my opponent was under immense pressure. He was tiring fast and had nowhere to go as I shadowed his back-pedalling.

I was now confidently staying close and using my speed to duck under and evade any punches coming my way, enabling me to deliver close, telling body hooks that were taking his breath away.

His normal advantages had suddenly become his biggest disadvantages. His long arms were now ineffective as I fought up close, never leaving a space between us far enough away for him to deliver any worthwhile punches. Even his immaculate footwork had become useless as I hounded him.

I was back into that flowing motion that I was so used to, where each punch I delivered set me up for the next one. I was always in the right position to deliver the telling punches that came from just a simple left or right hip twist. The results I was after were starting to show.

It's a great feeling when you're performing well and in control, like a well-rehearsed dance between footwork, balance and poise: a controlled sequence of fast non-stop punching that was having a positive effect for me.

Aggressive and ruthless, but necessary.

The hours and hours of relentless punching during training on the heavy bag was now more than ever providing dividends.

The second round came to an abrupt end; I had him cowering in his own corner, hammering his body. All I could hear, even above the crowd, was the noise from his grunts and his corner screaming at him to grab hold. Well, that's what it sounded like, but in Welsh!

I could see the smile on Jimmy's face as I made my way back to my corner. No rush, I wasn't tired. I was now in full control, confident that more of the same for the next round would bring in the result I was after.

As the bell sounded for the final round, I could tell immediately, even before I moved across towards him, that he had been instructed to keep me at arm's length. His jabs were constantly being pushed out far more frequently than necessary. But he was jabbing at thin air most of the time in an attempt to keep a substantial space between us. Fast at first, but then fizzling out to a whimper, as I caught him with a couple of heavy body hooks. He was quickly tiring.

After less than half a minute of punching and missing, I could see the frustration on his face. Patience was paying off and it was now time to let loose again.

His lightning-fast jabs and fleet footwork of the first round had slowed down to punches that were easy to deal with. This relatively slow-moving target became the sign I was looking for.

With just over a minute to go, moving forward I slipped a slower incoming left jab over my right shoulder and with just a slight twist from the hips caught him under the ribs with a cracking left hook. My whole body was on the move forward as the punch connected; together with his incoming action, the power of my punch was multiplied, becoming a sort of double impact.

His legs buckled and, gasping for breath, he sank to the canvas onto his knees. The fight was stopped immediately. I was directed to a natural corner, whilst both the referee and his trainer helped my opponent to his feet and worked to bring his breathing under control.

A very hostile crowd had suddenly become a very appreciative crowd, giving me rousing applause and a huge cheer as it was announced by the Master of Ceremonies, in a very Welsh voice, that I had won on a TKO. My opponent was unable to carry on.

As instructed, I waited in my corner and was delighted to be introduced to the one and only Jimmy Wilde.

This Welsh boxing legend, nicknamed 'The Mighty Atom' or the 'Tylertown Terror', was the son of a coal miner, a pit boy himself and arguably the greatest UK fighter ever. At his peak, weighing in at 112lbs (just above my own fighting weight), Jimmy was crowned the first-ever world-champion flyweight. His credentials include over 139 professional wins, including ninety-nine KOs, just three losses and nine no contest, which probably means draws.

Yet here was a sixty-year-old Jimmy who stood before me, now looking like an old man who had let himself go. Much shorter than me now, looking more like a barrel than the legend he once was as, he came over to congratulate me. He had entered the ring to announce my win, during which he received several boisterous comments from the crowd, mainly about the weight he was now carrying.

One loud heckler created a huge uproar, shouting, 'Who's thi' butcher then, Jimmy?' I didn't understand his answer in native Welsh, but from the laughter around the hall I gathered it must have been funny.

Jimmy Wilde shook my gloved hand and we shared a few minutes together in the ring whilst my opponent recovered. He then followed me out of the ring through the cheering crowd to my changing room.

We sat for the best part of an hour whilst he reminisced about his colourful boxing career, both home and abroad.

Inquisitive about his career, he answered all my questions. I was fascinated, just listening to him talk in his deep Welsh voice about his long trips around Europe and beyond. An amazing guy who was able to use his skills to escape the dangers of the mine that had employed his family. He, like me, could remember most of his fights. Not bad for an old man.

Wait a minute! I have just realised I called Jimmy Wilde an old man at sixty and I am a month over eighty as I write this. Does that make me ancient? I certainly don't feel old, but now I'm wondering if that's how people see me, a wrinkly old man with a long-gone best-by date?

I have just completed twenty press-ups to make me feel good about myself. Still got it!

I digress.

We had missed our train connection home and were invited to stay in a hotel close by.

After a good night's sleep and an early breakfast, we were driven to the large railway station and managed to board an early morning train that, after just two changes, arrived back to Rotherham by mid-afternoon.

My cornerman, Jimmy, and I had both been made welcome, well looked after and were invited back. But that was the first and last time I would ever fight in Cardiff, a great experience nonetheless with wonderful memories.

I gave myself the weekend off, but it was good to get back to the gym the following Tuesday and discuss the Cardiff fight in detail with both Jimmy and Jacky.

An autopsy, so to speak, was carried out after every fight or experience worthy of learning from. Jimmy outlined to Jacky the opponent I had faced in Cardiff, together with details about the change of approach after the first round and, of course, the end result. We all agreed that the right instructions had been made which in turn had resulted in the success.

Had I learned from this experience? Jacky asked. Yes, I had, and I was happy with the fight, apart from the one little niggle I had shouting at me from my inner voice. It was telling me that I should have been able to analyse the problem and make that decision for myself during the first round, once I had realised I was being out-boxed and wouldn't win without changing tactics.

Was I being super critical? No, I don't think so. Being scrupulously analytical is equally as important, I feel, as learning how to box.

Over the next couple of months, I trained harder and spent more time on quickening my reaction speed, often sparring with two younger boys in the ring with me at the same time – and on occasions with my hands tucked in my shorts behind me.

Let me tell you this. When you have four gloved hands coming at you, all at the same time, with two young lads who knew that I wouldn't be punching back, well, I can tell you they were climbing over one another to let fly with punches. My reactions needed to be pretty sharp. Great training indeed.

It was about this time that my twelve-year-old younger brother Alan had decided he wanted to join me and become a boxer. Whilst I thought it was great, Mum on the other hand wasn't so keen. She was having enough sleepless nights over one of her sons, never mind two of us, she said.

It was great to be able to spend a good deal of time sparring and helping Alan to shape his southpaw (left-handed) stance. Something to occupy my time during this drought of competition.

We set about training and getting him ready for his first competitive fight in Sheffield city centre.

Alan was always going to be a fighter but never a boxer; he also didn't like training hard. However, he packed one of the most powerful punches I had encountered, as I found out during many hours of sparring around with one another. His awkward southpaw style was definitely one of his major assets.

Never one for spectator sports, I found it extremely frustrating to attend boxing tournaments just supporting our team fighters, both locally and out of South Yorkshire. But I did have an ulterior motive now with Alan. Even though I wasn't fighting on these bills, I could give him all my support and guidance, steering him through any pitfalls during his first few fights.

Alan's first fight at Pitsmoor Working Men's Club in Sheffield was a huge success. Although he got caught a few times, he did stop his young opponent in the third round.

His second fight at Southey Green Working Men's Club, also in Sheffield, followed much the same pattern. A win again on a TKO in the second round, although Alan did sustain some facial punishment. But he was quite content to lead with his nose, so to speak.

Even though I was more than concerned for my younger brother's lack of boxing skills, he seemed happy enough to take a handful of punches if it meant he could deliver his cracking powerful left hook. Somewhat different to his older brother, who definitely didn't like being hit – at all!

It's good for team morale and encouraging for the younger fighters, I was told, as I was being asked more and more to supervise and look after them during tournaments. It was around this time I became an occasional coach and took charge during some of the fights, with Jacky looking on.

I enjoyed the responsibility of providing advice, of giving accurate instructions in between rounds that had positive conclusions during fights for the young boys in my charge. It reminded me of the way my two coaches, Benny and Jacky, had steered me to wins.

But my first love was to compete. I loved to fight and,

although it was great to give something back, I was becoming increasingly frustrated with boxing or, to be fair, the lack of it.

6

Don't look, Maureen

Mark Twain once famously commented, 'The two most important days in your life are the day you are born and the day you find out why.'

Two of the sincerest of comments I have ever made over the past twenty years are, 'I will never allow age to become an obstacle and never allow my ageing body to stop me achieving dreams,' and, 'The difference between the possible and the impossible often lies between our own two ears.'

As I write this, possibly my last book, those classic Ray Matthews comments now seem a bit unrealistic going forward as these Covid-19 pandemic restrictions bite, reshaping our new way of life and holding vice-like the foreseeable global future.

Gripped firmly in one of the scariest periods of my whole life – and believe me, it takes a lot to scare me – I am only ever scared of things I can't see. This horrible pandemic is certainly scary and has ravaged the lives of many of my friends, colleagues and relations, turning the world on its head and causing me to re-evaluate the remaining years of my life, however long that may be.

It's now more imperative than ever, I believe, to deliberate and evaluate a new set of values, causing me to look more carefully at what is important in my life and also consider what will satisfy me for the remaining time that I have left. The world we lived in will never be quite the same and we will need to come to terms with the new normal, I believe.

Looking back, I have lived and enjoyed a full and interesting life that has provided fantastic memories. Memories that still fire me up like a shot in the arm, as I recall the many challenges that needed courage at the time, or possibly insanity, to take on. That depends on your interpretation, I suppose.

*

Join me again as I continue to reminisce about the wildest dream I've had to date, the birthday challenge of those seventy-five consecutive marathons.

We were on a roll. Day after day the miles were stacking up and this wrinkly, seventy-five-year-old body was coping admirably as each marathon ended in another great memory. It was even better than I had ever dared to dream about during all those months of preparation and concern.

My weight was stable and constant at around ten stone, thanks to Barry, and, other than a tight hamstring, which I was due to have checked over with Kay later that afternoon, I was full of confidence. Smiley faces all round.

But let's face it, no matter how confident I was about physically smashing this challenge, I couldn't allow complacency to take over, even though I had the best team possible to keep me mobile. After all, having entered into the unknown, there was always that risk-factor element that the collective team hadn't even thought about.

I was in no real rush to complete the daily marathons. I'd decided I would treat each day as though I was going out to work. This challenge was not a race but more like a job, even though it was nine years since I had set foot on a building site to earn a living; retirement just before my sixty-seventh birthday had opened up a whole new world.

Long before the marathons began, I had received a phone call from the founder and organiser of that year's Brinsworth 10K, Mark Robinson, asking me if I would enter and run. The ever-popular local road race was now in its seventh year and Mark wanted me to be there on the start line.

'I am sure we could work your race into the second marathon,' I remember answering, as it coincided with the second marathon on Sunday 3rd July.

That would be the very first time I'd be actually taking part in the Brinsworth race, having helped out by marshalling the event every year from its conception.

After working out the logistics, it soon became evident that it would be a great opportunity to increase the profile of both the 10K for Mark, as well as my marathon challenge and help me to promote the fundraising message.

What made this invite even more special was that Mark's wife, Joanna, is a teacher at Newman School. She would also play a major role in the organisation of my final marathon, where I would be running into the school grounds.

The event was then booked in on the sponsor calendar page before any other company could claim that date.

The advertisement in our local press and flyers from the race about my taking part in the Brinsworth 10K had the desired results, bringing in a good sum of money from the runners and spectators. Mark would also be donating a large percentage of the profits from the event to our Golden Giving sponsor page.

I had worked out the mileage using Google Maps. If I was to run from my home in Maltby to the race start line in Brinsworth, take part in the race and then run home through Whiston, passing Newman School, it worked out to around twenty-seven miles. Perfect for the second marathon.

On the morning of Sunday 3rd July, having already completed just under ten miles, I arrived on the start line in plenty of time, receiving a fantastic reception from local club athletes and from people whom I had never met before but who were familiar with my challenge.

What a fabulous experience throughout the race, surrounded by enthusiastic athletes running alongside me for most of the race, with supporting crowds and marshals cheering me on along the streets around the western side of Brinsworth and Catcliffe.

As the race came to its final stages, climbing the steep bank from Brinsworth Road following the roped area, I was escorted through the cordoned-off entrance onto the large school playing field which brought out a very enthusiastic announcement from over the loudspeaker, shouting my name.

'Come on, Ray, you're looking good, mate!' A most humbling experience, as everyone cheered.

During the final stage of the 10K race, whilst I was following the roped track around the perimeter of the field,

I was suddenly surrounded by a large group of cheering children who had taken part in their own race earlier on. They joined me to run the last couple of hundred yards through the finish line into a large cheering crowd of supporters.

Later, I was honoured to present the winning trophies to the 2016 winners. Ross Floyd, all the way from Northumberland, was the first across the finish line, winning that year's event in an incredible time for the course of 32.37. Gemma Woodhead, a more local runner, ran through the finish line as winner of the ladies' race in an equally impressive time of 41.02.

What an amazing end to the race, but that wasn't the end of running for me. After saying my goodbyes and thanks for a very memorable event, I headed off for home to complete the second marathon.

I was on a high, leaving most of my running friends to celebrate in the Three Magpies pub.

Sorry, guys, I would love to have joined the after-race celebration party.

The bigger picture was far more important. Maureen answered the phone on the second ring as I headed off down the road. She would have my meat and two veg Sunday dinner ready and waiting, as arranged.

With 28.66 miles showing on my Garmin watch, I turned the corner into my drive and, just over six hours since I left my home, the second marathon came to an end.

I was starving and, after a long, hot, soothing shower, it was time for fuelling and filling up the tank with a big Sunday roast dinner.

The weather was kind over the coming weeks and I was running comfortably, recovering well, and feeling more and more confident. As each day went by, my belief grew that I had not taken on an impossible challenge.

There was much time to ponder and reflect during mile after mile of plodding through street and countryside during my new way of life. Much of that headspace was filled with the realisation of how that seventy-five marathons dream, originally a birthday present to me to satisfy a whim, had escalated into magnificent proportions from which hundreds of children would benefit.

The staggering amount of £75,000 that I needed to raise for Newman School had completely changed the status of my challenge and spurred me on day after day to achieve the target.

The new daily routine of my life soon became more of a habit and many marathons were completed by starting out from home in the mornings, running around the very familiar trails, paths and roads that I had trained around over the years, and finishing at home in time for dinner mid-afternoon.

I would head out in different directions, mostly clocking up well over marathon distances. In fact, the time each marathon was taking to complete became longer, as more and more people recognised me out running and wanted autographs or a selfie or even just a chat. Although this was a bit of a chore at times, I was never in a rush to finish these daily marathons in the first place, so these small diversions helped to ensure extra public response and bring in additional money.

I was booked in for and looking forward to the ninth marathon, with Clowne Road Runners as main sponsors.

All the arrangements had been made weeks ago through

an old friend of mine and active club member, Richard Hind, whom I'd bumped into during a number of local races in the past.

When Richard found out about my unusual challenge, he had secured the ninth marathon on behalf of Clowne Road Runners. Richard was a long-time member of this cracking running club, one which boasted many talented runners and hosted various club and open races themselves.

Arrangements had been made to meet Richard and a group of club runners at the Arkwright Community Centre on the outskirts of Bolsover, Chesterfield, which happens to be just a few hundred yards away from the Trans-Pennine trail.

Using this old redundant light railway line as part of a 5.2-mile loop turned out to be a pretty good idea. The disused light railway track, now used by runners, walkers and cyclists, where we would be mostly running proved to be fairly flat, kind on the feet and limbs with a traffic-free bonus.

Richard had worked out that we needed to complete the loop five times and then make up the rest of the mileage by extending the last lap beyond the starting point before doubling back to the finish.

A great distance runner himself, Richard totally understood and had commented that the less I had to think or worry about during our time together on this ninth marathon, the better experience I would have. True.

I had been looking forward to this marathon since it was arranged; just running and following other runners meant that I could totally relax and chill out.

It was great to be supported with this mixed group of Clowne runners, which also included Richard's wife, Gemma, their youngest daughter Molly on her bike and her elder sister Daisy on foot, who was a little star throughout the marathon. I wasn't surprised to see regular racegoers Paul Sommerly, Gareth and Louise Lowe, as well as Freya, Amelia and Ben Lowe. The enthusiastic group also included Karen Shipman, Dave and Julie Keeling, who were all gathered on the start line awaiting my arrival.

We were met at the start area by the local press reporter, who disappeared before we got underway, although just over a week later there was a very informative article in the *Derbyshire Times* about the challenge, some background and a great photo of our group. This was not the first time that the *Times* had reported on my challenges; they had picked up on my 150-mile run and reported on the trike presentation four years earlier.

We set off into the drizzle that had been with us since before arriving at the centre, down the eight-foot-wide tree-lined trail. Luckily the weather didn't get any worse, which made for very pleasant running conditions. I personally love running in the rain.

We could hear loud music in the distance within half an hour of setting off, then again about four miles into the 5.2-mile loop as we skirted around to our right, leaving the trail behind. It turned out to be a local fair that was in full swing, taking up a large amount of the field and path that had been ear-marked as part of the route. However, a short detour soon had us returning onto the track and back up to the start area to complete lap one of the five.

Before turning back out again, some of the running group, waving their goodbyes and shouts of good luck, left after the first lap, with others following suit after the second.

Other members of the club, including Chris Lane and Catlin Hazlehurst, joined during the latter part of the marathon.

As we headed out past the start line at the end of the last loop, my watch was now showing just over twenty-four miles.

New faces had joined our now smaller group and, in order to make up the remainder of the minimum 26.2 miles needed to complete marathon number nine, we set off on this new section of the route. To be honest, this wet, slippery path was not great for running on.

The path had become boggy and a complete change from the flat, well-consolidated Trans-Pennine Trail we had run most of the earlier miles on. For the first time I had reservations about the uneven trail, conscious of twisting an ankle or taking a dive in the mud.

We were all now headed in the opposite direction to make up the miles, out into the up-and-down rough, muddy terrain that looked more akin to trail bike-riding than marathon-running. Despite that, less than half an hour later, we made the turn and all ran through the finish line, resulting in an overall distance of 26.31 miles. The closest I would ever achieve to the actual marathon distance.

After coffee and nibbles at the Arkwright Centre, I headed for home up the M1, windscreen-wiper blades still in big demand.

The life of a marathon runner is mostly about managing those little niggles before they turn into problems and can often be dealt with whilst running. There's also this ongoing dialogue that takes place in your head when you're questioning your sanity, and it really is OK to talk to yourself. The big problem comes when you start to answer yourself back and you don't win the argument!

What I am trying to say is that, in reality, it's how you deal with these issues that make the difference between failure and success over long-distance running.

Another one bites the dust.

Just after breakfast, a few days later, the phone rang. It turned out to be Nicola from Look North checking how the marathons were going. I recognised her voice this time!

'Other than the shortage of pound notes coming in fast enough, I'm delighted,' I responded. 'Everything is on track running-wise and I'm feeling good and strong.'

'Then it's time we got together again and gave your challenge a bit of a boost. Can I come and do some live filming for the 6:30pm news slot today? If we could meet around five o'clock, we could do some filming and then set up for the live link later. Where would be a good place to film?' she said.

As luck would have it, she had just caught me as I was due to set off to run the thirteenth marathon that would take in the picturesque Langold Lake in Worksop. The route would make for great footage, I suggested.

'Can you get some of your running club mates to agree to being filmed with you?' she asked.

Hell's bells! I was sure I could, but she wasn't giving me much time to organise myself, never mind my mates! After a few more questions about the state of my health, she further requested that it would be good if I could get Barry to come along and answer a couple of questions about the daily nutritional input.

'Oh, and this time I will have the outside broadcasting van with me. Can you check that I will be able to access the lakeside?' Nicola asked. 'This will be going out live.'

At last, one of those big vans with the dishes that I had visions about earlier. A proper job this time!

Following quick phone calls to some of my running club

mates and a further request on Facebook for volunteers, I had secured enough of my running club colleagues and friends to make up a quorum. Barry had also agreed to attend and be interviewed to discuss my dietary requirements.

The day's marathon was pretty much completed by the time I arrived at Langold Lake around 5pm. Here I was joined by a larger group of friends and running club colleagues than I had expected. Had they all turned up to support me, or was their attendance in the hope they'd be on telly?

After exchanging pleasantries and collating the list of names, Nicola informed the group how she wanted the filming to play out. She made a start at setting up the much larger camera, this time on the wide tarmac path at the southern end overlooking the lake. A pretty substantial tripod stand, with the "furry rat" sound microphone attached to one of the legs, was used this time.

The afternoon sun was beginning to settle low over the tree line at the far end of the lake, casting a reddish tint across the water. Should look great for the live broadcast, I was thinking, as Nicola began instructing the group on what she wanted from them.

We were all invited to go through the actions of running towards her as a group from the direction of the derelict swimming pool around four hundred yards away.

'Don't look at the camera. Just run straight past for a few yards,' she advised as we left her to head for our start line.

With the lake in the background, on signal, Brian and Barbara Lounds, Bob Houghton, Matthew Asbridge, Caroline Boyd, Steph and Cuma Celic, and John Proffitt ran, with me leading, towards Nicola and then past the camera for a yard or two.

'That's great,' she said.

Then it was my turn to repeat the process on my own, but this time my colleagues, who were now stood lakeside, were asked to provide a rousing cheer as I passed, with Jim Southern in attendance taking club photos.

Nicola had picked up on the initial weight-loss issue I had experienced early doors and, during the face-to-face interview with Barry, expressed her concern for my health.

As a runner herself, Nicola was finding it hard to understand how I was not experiencing any adverse problems with my day-to-day marathons, or at least suffering with fatigue or some form of muscle damage.

Now just over 320 miles in and still going strong, she mentioned that viewers' sympathy would probably help to bring in more money if I was seen to be struggling a bit. 'Might be a good idea not to mention how good you feel,' she suggested.

During the live link, Nicola steered the conversation around to my initial weight loss and the dangerous implications if it were to continue into more marathons. But we concluded that I was feeling positive and still expecting to hit both targets – completing seventy-five marathons and raising £75,000 for Newman School with the help of our viewers.

The live broadcast was a huge success, easily measured by the increased activity we experienced on our Golden Giving fundraising page over the following days.

We said our goodbyes with a promise to get together in the near future. 'I have an idea for our next interview. What about a visit to your doctors – can you set something up for our next filming in Maltby?' Nicola asked.

The power of the media is immense.

Dr Khan readily agreed and accepted that the publicity would be good for his practice and, of course, I was more than happy to help as he had always been wholeheartedly behind my running challenges over the years. He had been more than helpful when I had been in need of a doctor's Certification of Fitness to fulfil the requirements of entry for some of my previous races overseas.

A few days after speaking to Nicola, I was travelling up the M1, heading for Hoyland, to yet another appointment with Kay Atkin, marathon team physio and long-serving member of Pure Physiotherapy. I was accompanied by that week's niggles and information charts on the seat beside me.

Kay, a former Olympic physio, was due to straighten out a few knots that had jumped up and bit me a few times over the last couple of days. Mainly the old hamstring attachment at my right buttock.

I was also delivering a few days' worth of completed fact sheets that she had designed. These fact sheets were nothing more than a simple questionnaire filled in by just a tick on the appropriate facial expression. This provided a visual commentary on my moods, sleep pattern, state of health and fitness that I had experienced during that day.

The faces ranged from a huge grin down to a very sad image that I had to choose from to symbolise how I felt as I woke each morning, during the day and just before going to bed.

Over the years, Kay and Pure Physiotherapy have kept me on the go by successfully looking after my many damaged ligaments and muscles. I was thankful they were once again on board providing physiotherapy expertise when needed day or night.

Kay was waiting in reception and no sooner had I entered the clinic door than I was invited into her treatment room to lie face down on the couch.

Those all-too-familiar fingers were soon hard at work and, once she had found 'the spot,' she set about manipulating the offending tendons.

I am always happy to endure the different kinds of pain those probing fingers dealt out, knowing that when treatment finally ended the results would always turn out the same – comfort. Comfort from the original pain, the results of hours of over-used tight tendons.

Before she had finished, Kay passed me a medium-sized box and suggested I try the contents, as she talked me through the instructions. Inside was a Body Pro, an electric-powered vibrating massager, designed to provide soft tissue relief for muscles through six vibrating pads. Strategically placed, these pads would aid muscle recovery day after day.

'It could be useful if you use it after you've had your bath. I have secured this for you to use till you've completed your marathons,' Kay said as I left for home.

How lucky I was to have such an unselfish dedicated member of the team providing expert skills that would help to ensure that I could continue to perform day after day and achieve my goal. A thank-you hardly ever seemed enough.

In an effort to add a bit of something different to the more mundane marathons, I suggested to Maureen that it would be great if she would accompany me during one of the marathons. We decided to complete the twenty-third marathon together as that one hadn't been allocated or sponsored.

It would give us an opportunity to spend some precious

time together, after three weeks of me being out running most of the day.

As we would be out in the immense forestry area of Clumber Park, owned and maintained by the National Trust on the outskirts of Worksop, Nottinghamshire, we decided to take a picnic and split the marathon into two halves to make a day of it.

The southern tip of Clumber Park is a much-frequented area for quiet seclusion and we would be able to make full use of the flattish cycle route number six which forms part of over twenty miles of off-road cycling and running routes within the park. It would be perfect for Maureen to ride alongside me on her bike for the first half-marathon distance, then a change of direction after a spot of lunch. We'd agreed to complete the remainder of the marathon in and around nearby Sherwood Forest. The day was planned to perfection.

I suppose it's very difficult to ride at the slow, steady pace I was running, because Maureen had to stop and wait for me to catch up a few times. However, just over two hours later after a most enjoyable just over thirteen miles clocked up, we arrived back at the car to have lunch.

Bread and blackcurrant jam sandwiches for me and an energy bar, washed down with a reyt nice cuppa Yorkshire tea.

Half an hour later and feeling refreshed, we locked the car and headed across the B6034 road, down the number six cycle route towards Sherwood Forest, aka Robin Hood country.

On the first section of the downhill path, due to its narrowness, I was able to keep Maureen behind so that my marathon legs wouldn't have to be keeping up with her at track speed.

After about quarter of an hour on this track through the

dense woodland, we came to a sudden halt at the main road. We waited in bewilderment to cross, for a good five minutes, as streams of cars were turning into the track we were heading for. Eventually we managed to cross the road, following the convoy of cars as they travelled down the path ahead of us before disappearing out of sight into Sherwood Forest.

'I can't understand where all those cars are going to, there's only an old water-pumping station less than a quarter of a mile down this track,' I said to Maureen, who was now leading the way.

But two or three minutes later I could see in the distance a line of about thirty cars parked up on the right of the path with boot lids opened and what looked like nude figures glowing in the afternoon sun.

As we got nearer, and now confirming what I thought I saw, they were definitely a large gathering of nude men and women lined up in front of their cars, almost blocking our path through.

'Don't look, Maureen!'

'Now this is not something you see every day,' I thought to myself as I continued to run, with the biggest grin on my face past the line of parked cars, acknowledging their enthusiastic hellos!

A couple of Fords, loads of Toyotas, Jags, Vauxhalls, three Fiats. Who am trying to kid? Who looks at makes of cars in these unbelievable circumstances?

These men and women, completely bollock-naked, were proudly displaying some incredible sights. Some big guys and even bigger gals were waving excitedly and shouting their hellos, making wobbly bits wobble even more. My goodness, what a sight!

Just before reaching the end of this most unusual gathering of birthday-suited humans, I heard a crash ahead of me. As I turned my head round (my eyes had obviously been transfixed on these jaunty sights to my right), I could see Maureen crumpled in a heap, her bike on top and looking like it was about to devour her.

She had crashed into the pedestrian barriers that were in place to stop vehicles getting through.

I hotfooted it the last twenty yards and untangled her from the bike and post, both of us in hysterical fits of laughter.

I dusted her down and, once dignity had been restored, we set off into Sherwood Forest still laughing for the next few miles.

Oh, the bike's OK, by the way.

In all that excitement, I had completely forgot to check the mileage on my Garmin, being otherwise engaged in fits of laughter and speculations as to what this gaggle of nudists were up to. I suddenly realised that we needed to be heading back or this marathon would end up a pure Ultra.

'Which way are we going back?' asked Maureen.

'The same way,' I shouted as we made the turn just short of the great Major Oak.

The bare-bottomed group were not waiting for us, or anywhere in sight, as we headed back. Looks like they were in the woods doing whatever nude people do in woods.

They did have boots on, I think. I wasn't really looking at their feet.

'Now then, if I had come home today and told you what we had just seen, you wouldn't have believed a word of it, would you?' I asked Maureen.

'Probably not,' she replied with a chuckle.

What an eventful marathon it had turned out to be. I was definitely not taking Maureen on any more marathons; the excitement was far too much for a mere marathon runner to cope with.

*

Guest Contribution

Kay Atkin, team physio

I'm indebted to Kay for all that she contributed to the challenge. From the thorough preparation to the ad-hoc 'running repairs', she has been an integral part of the support team. I even had my own 'hotline', but you'll read about that later!

Ray Matthews

I first found out about Ray's seventy-five challenge when he called me to let me know that my boss, Phin, had agreed that Pure Physiotherapy would do whatever was required to support him. The thing was, Phin was in Norwich and I was in Yorkshire, so Ray kindly updated me so I was fully aware of the immense challenge ahead.

By this time, I had been treating Ray intermittently since around 2011, gradually taking over from Phin after his move to Norwich.

I have always liked a challenge so I was more than happy to assist with this one – despite the sudden realisation hitting me that this was a mammoth task. Not just in terms of the length of the challenge of seventy-five consecutive days, which equates to two and a half months' continuous cover, but also the unknown entity of how the body structures would respond to the massive demand. Also to be considered were the lack of rest days and the complexity of 'agedness'. Ray will kill me for that, but it sounds slightly better than geriatric.

Upon the acceptance of supporting Ray during the challenge, I hit the research button. I was aware of a lot of elite sport rehabilitation and preventative rehabilitation from my time working with GB athletes. I had undertaken an MSc in that very topic. However, there was nothing to be found on endurance events for Ray's age group.

A physio's work is definitely not just at the time of the event. There were many, many months of preparation leading up to the event, as well as the time following the event, as you cannot run a marathon every day for seventy-five days then just stop!

I had attended a few courses prior to Ray's event and bumped into some old colleagues from my days at the English Institute of Sport. The great thing in physio is that colleagues are always happy to collaborate and knowledge-share. Now, although again there was no 'how-to' guide for this, even these discussions were useful and helped me sound-board my thought process at the time.

We were also fortunate that BodyFlow agreed to loan Ray a machine to assist with his recovery during the event. I had utilised this electrotherapy device whilst working in sport; it was originally developed to help with lymphedema and swelling but was also found to be great for sports recovery – and I believe certainly freed up some of my evenings by reducing the need for soft-tissue recovery work.

The action plan was to work with Ray in the lead-up to the event and build a 'toolkit' of things that he found useful. As physios, we have our 'toolkit' of many different techniques and treatment methods which we pick and choose from as we treat different patients. What I wanted to do for Ray was build one for him, where we had tried and tested the different treatment techniques, so we didn't end up using something new in the middle of the challenge.

More importantly, Ray had the psychological buy-in to the treatment, knowing it had had a previous positive effect, which by the power of the mind makes it more likely to be effective when used at that critical moment that we hoped would never occur mid-challenge.

A few weeks prior to the start date, Ray suffered a flare-up of a long-standing problem. Over many years Ray has suffered with pain at the base of the buttock (technical name proximal hamstring insertional tendinopathy), some irritation of the hamstring tendon where it attaches to the bone of the pelvis.

Now tendons are funny things – they don't like change! This is the ramping up of load but also ramping down loading too quickly. I do remember about two weeks from the start, Ray was determined to take a full week off to give the tendon a rest, as it wasn't settling as quickly as we had hoped. I was internally nearly having a breakdown, thinking, 'I have no chance if you just stop everything.'

However, after lots and lots of educational discussions, Ray agreed to stick with the plan and we both took a deep breath and stopped panicking. Time was not on our side at this point, but luckily, very luckily, it calmed down and we got him on the starting line, fit and symptom-free.

The first few days went without problems, despite me

becoming the jumpiest person every time my phone rang. By day three, I decided to change my ringtone and allocated Ray his own tune. This meant I knew if it was a general call or if it was Ray. It didn't, however, stop me jumping if Ray's ringtone went off. My patients at the time were all very understanding and were aware the challenge was happening, encouraging me to answer the call if he had rung through during their treatment.

Around day five Ray contacted me to advise he had stubbed his big toe on a tree branch. Luckily, the toolkit came in useful, as we had tested varying taping methods during the months prior to the event to see which he found comfortable and least restrictive. This allowed me to tape and support the joint which was injured whilst Ray had the mental confidence that it wouldn't hinder his running.

The day after, my phone rang mid-morning and I was all ready to jump in the car and race to wherever Ray was in his marathon. However, it was a quick call, whilst enjoying his blackcurrant jam sandwiches, to let me know the toe was feeling better than he had expected and the tape had done the trick. Panic over!

Now at the time the challenge was taking place, I had already got a few things in the diary. There were some birthdays and family events that had been on the calendar for ages. Ray had a rough idea of when I was around and was always very accommodating and would come to the particular clinic I was at during that day after his marathon. Alternatively, we would try to pre-plan in some of the sessions to reduce the chance of a call-out. However, I did emphasise that he needed to keep me in the loop, and if ever needed, I would return to one of the clinics to see him.

During one weekend, I was down in Lincoln when a call came through. A quick dash back to the Rotherham clinic on the Saturday evening, a bit of release work on some tight, tired legs and Ray was good to go the next day, and I headed back to the family gathering. I must admit I had expected a number of dashes. However, I can only really recall this one.

As the challenge progressed there became increasing interest from the press. ITV and BBC Look North had both started covering the challenge. The time had come where Ray had organised a televised interview which was to take place during a physio session at our Hoyland clinic.

A physio is the support team, not a lead role. We hide in the background, behind the scenes, keeping the cogs turning so the main machine can function. I was not used to being interviewed whilst trying to treat a patient. I kept reminding myself, 'Think before you speak.' Not always my best quality, as I often just say what I'm thinking. I remember them re-shooting sections of the interview and saying Ray did not look in enough pain, telling me to just 'dig in a little more'. Fortunately, Ray managed to add some acting to the mix, rather than me increasing the torture!

The other side of the increased press interest was the nightly updates on the news. I remember a comment about Ray not being like everyone else (because he isn't!) and he wasn't looking tired enough, etc., as most of us would be crawling after one marathon, let alone seventy-five!

However, on this particular day around 5pm, feeding time at the zoo in my house, I had a few repeat calls from Ray. Now this confused me as I had already spoken to him earlier and he had completed the marathon for the day. The call went along the lines of, 'Don't panic when you watch the news. Yes, I did trip over, but it really was not as dramatic as they are making out.'

Given the fact Ray had felt the need to call made me turn on the news to see what the fuss was about. Ray's side of the story: there was a stick that had fallen across the track, he had taken a tumble, got up and carried on without any issue. The news reader's side of the story: there was a tree root that he got caught up with and went rolling off the path, but he still managed to limp his way around the rest of the marathon.

Once we reached the halfway mark, I really felt that, at this point, Ray could get to the end. It had felt like if something had gone wrong during the early days that it would have been far too long to limp someone through to reach the end. There was also a very high likelihood I would have had to have the difficult conversation about withdrawing from the challenge. I had prepared myself for this but had hoped I wouldn't need to.

Ray has a mentality that would drive him through, so long as we could keep the physical side going. My biggest worry was the lack of rest days, as there was zero recovery time throughout the event.

Despite the enormity of the challenge, the final day seemed to come around really quickly.

I had planned on running the last mile with Ray with 'Fred', our friendly skeleton, who we had had some fun with over the last couple of months. However, it fell on a day I didn't have childcare so instead had the little ones, aged three and one at the time. They, however, thought it was great as the grass was freshly cut in the Newman School grounds and there was a little embankment that they could crawl up and roll back down, covered in grass cuttings.

There was no mistaking when the runners drew near; the noise, cheers and the huge truck that had caused plenty of disruption to traffic on the final route down to Newman School.

It was very emotional seeing Ray finally crossing the finish line with the accompanying relief that the challenge had finally been completed.

I don't think until that point I had realised the anxiety I had in the back of my mind throughout. It was a very different event to covering a match or tournament. An endurance event is just that: endurance for the athlete and the support team. Even though it is not you doing the event, in the world of sport you give it your all and for me that is supporting my athlete/team with whatever is needed for the duration.

I remember after Ray crossed that finish line, seeking out his wife Maureen and telling her to make sure he went for a run tomorrow. Probably the last thing anyone would be thinking, but the taper-down after the event finished was important as this could be when all the little niggles raise their ugly heads and protest, if the load stepped down too quickly.

7

KO for anti-boxing campaigners

As I write about my early years, back in the forties, when I was a young, free and virtually unrestricted teenager, life skill learning became second nature. I reflect on the difference of the modern lifestyle of today's teenagers and shudder.

It's a fearsome thought that the rise in technology (which honestly scares me to death), particularly mobile phones and social media, is fuelling a growing epidemic of the sedentary, couch-bound lifestyles of our youth of today. Is it coincidence that mental health problems seem to have grown, out of all proportions, during the past few years?

Our generation spent their days outside, kicking a pig-skin bladder about on a patch of grass, or running around the streets playing "catch". Most children today appear much less active, enthralled by an online lifestyle which seems to have taken over the real world.

It therefore came as no surprise to learn that childhood obesity levels are on the rise again, with around twenty-two per cent of children in my local town overweight or even obese. This starts in our infant schools before children reach their fifth birthdays! By the time they're ready to leave primary school, the obesity levels have reached around thirty-six per cent – that's a terrifying number! Over one third of all eleven-year-olds are overweight or obese. What frightening statistics.

I believe we have a responsibility to educate our children how to activate a healthier lifestyle and it's freely available to everyone. Surely we can help raise the aspirational bar higher and inspire children to take up extra-curricular activities such as tennis, boxing, football, dance or anything else that tickles their fancies?

Every child grows differently and, of course, not all are overweight. However, increasing activity levels has far more benefits than just reducing childhood obesity levels. Improving their current lifestyles will set them up with the skills and mindset to enhance their own quality of life. Surely this is far preferable to just sitting around waiting for things to happen, or even worse, allowing their health to deteriorate beyond repair?

Over the past five years or so, I have been actively involved in championing 'Run a Mile a Day with Ray' in and around my hometown and beyond. Providing help and assistance to more than fifty-four schools has resulted in almost instant success.

This simple initiative is working. It's free to implement, takes no more than fifteen minutes, requires no special equipment and there's virtually no set-up time.

Our children's health is an investment for their future as they can only give their best if they are at their best, fit and healthy.

Encouraging comments from participating school headteachers have included, 'bullying has decreased or disappeared', 'our children are showing increased learning capabilities', 'our children are healthier and more settled'.

A further bonus that I hadn't even considered was, 'Even our teachers have benefited from the daily mile; they're now slimmer, fitter, healthier and delivering more enthusiastic lessons. It's just a win-win solution.'

These uplifting comments fuel my determination to continue because, as part of this challenge, I also encourage teachers to take part in the mile with the children.

I don't need a barometer to reassure me it will work. I know it will.

We need to invest in our children now. Not tomorrow, as that may be too late, if this national pattern continues without someone applying the brakes.

My big panoramic dream would be to have every school in Rotherham, South Yorkshire or even the country running a mile a day. Then we'll make a start on the parents and get them to leave their cars a mile away and run or walk with their kids to school. But don't say owt, they don't know that yet!

As an active ambassador for Age UK Rotherham, I am also looking to close the gap between the young and old in the community. I am doing this by dispelling the myth that there are certain activities that we just shouldn't be doing past a certain age, as has been intimated to me a number of times!

'What, at your age?'

How many times has that comment been levelled at me, over the latter years, when announcing a challenge that I would be taking on?

I really enjoy giving motivational talks to receptive, ageing people, knowing that it will make a difference to their health and wellbeing and being actively involved in fundraising.

*

Digression over!

My younger brother, Alan, was now starting to become established as a fighter. Slowly but surely, he had gained a local reputation for himself as a KO specialist, having stopped all his previous opponents before the end of the third round.

His fifth fight was coming up at Pitsmoor Working Men's Club in Sheffield. This would see him matched against their local Yorkshire schoolboy champion whom I had seen in action some months before.

My first reaction was that this was a complete mismatch; Alan's prospective opponent was far more experienced.

Although I was concerned for my brother, it did occur to me that this was the only way to make any sort of progress in the fight game. There's no shortcut, you have to fight better opponents in order to improve and advance.

A steady passage through his early competitive learning curve had been taken away from him, by virtue that he was winning so decisively, making it difficult to attract local club novices for him to fight against.

As I wouldn't be fighting on this local bill, I had been asked, and volunteered, to second in the club's corner with Jacky for this tournament. Six or seven of our boxers, aged between eleven and twenty-odd, would be representing the Phoenix Boxing Club.

I couldn't deny that I wasn't disappointed that I wasn't

fighting, but I had long since come to terms with the realisation that, until one of the local fighters at my weight (and there were plenty coming through the ranks) became more experienced and determined to take my scalp, I would have to keep travelling further afield to get matched up.

The brotherly feelings I was experiencing supporting Alan, from the other side of the ropes, were emotionally draining. I was now beginning to realise just what my mum had been going through whilst I had been fighting. She would have been worried sick every time I left the house to compete in a sport which, by definition, meant that someone could get hurt.

For the very first time in my life, I was experiencing serious concern for the welfare of one of my younger brothers.

Scary.

I'd never felt as nervous as I did when we left the gym and boarded the coach, with Alan leading the way looking like a seasoned pro. If he was nervous, then he was doing a great job of hiding it.

We set off just after teatime, 5:30ish, to make it in time to weigh in and get through the doctor's inspection before a start time of around 7:30pm. As usual, we entered the working men's club as a team with that air of professionalism we always created. They knew we'd arrived, that was for sure.

As the team settled down in our dressing room, I felt the need to let Alan have his own space and just kept out of his way, carrying on with my duties as the tournament started to get underway.

I'd worked out that Alan was scheduled to fight just before the first interval. It was impossible not keep checking that he was OK. God, I was a bag of nerves.

For the majority of the early fights, I was pre-occupied and keeping busy by learning the ropes as club second and experiencing the mid-round protocol.

One by one, our young boys were collected from our changing room and steered to the ring, as we steadily worked our way through the programme. Without exception, they all gave a great account of themselves. Three wins out of three, which added even greater weight on my younger brother to perform well. I knew he would be nervous and feeling the pressure.

Before long, it was time for me to lead Alan out through the avenue of seated spectators and awaiting crowd. I could feel the tension through his gloved hands as he made that long walk to the far corner and stepped into the ring, turning to face Jacky and me.

The referee summoned the two boys together shortly after Alan's opponent had entered the ring amid the cheering home crowd.

As they stood facing one another, either side of the referee, I could see the nods from them both as they were instructed of the dos and don'ts of what he required during the fight. He then signalled for them to return to their corners.

I had Alan's moist gum shield ready, handing it to Jacky as he walked back to us. I think, by this point, I had made the decision that I would never ever do this job again when it involved my young brother. I was a complete nervous wreck.

My usually steady hands were shaking as I passed a bottle of water for a mouth-rinse and I forgot to have the bucket ready for him to spit into.

'Come on, Ray, get your act together,' I silently gave myself a thorough rollicking.

Jacky, calm as ever, gave Alan some instructions and, as the bell sounded for the first round, exited the corner apron. He put his hand on my shoulder and gave me a squeeze as he settled by my side to watch. I knew he could feel my anxiety as we watched Alan make his start.

A great opening minute turned into a masterclass lesson in boxing, as Alan back-peddled for the rest of the round trying to cover up and avoid an onslaught from his more experienced opponent, which he was unable to deal with.

This boy could box and was able to control Alan with fast and telling left jabs that were scoring heavily, bringing up red welts around Alan's face.

I was praying for the bell to bring this one-sided first round to an end so that we – well, I mean Jacky – could give him the advice he so badly needed for round two.

Alan was never going to be a boxer. I had long since stopped trying to teach him the noble art of self-defence during our sparring sessions together. He always led with his nose, so to speak, but had a powerful left hand that normally would be the weapon his previous opponents couldn't deal with. But, in this round, it was proving to be of no use whatsoever because my brother couldn't get near enough to put it to use.

The round came to an end; I listened to Jacky's calm but intense instructions while Alan was settled on the stool that I had just remembered in time to place in our corner. Hell's bells, come on, Ray, get your act together. I was supposed to be the calm one.

'Don't let him push you around clockwise, you're walking onto his right hand,' Jacky had said. As a southpaw, Alan should be working his opponent anti-clockwise and setting himself up for his left cross or hooks; we had spent hours working on this basic instruction for him. There is, however, a massive difference between sparring with a brother and fighting in competition.

'Step across him and get inside those left jabs. Let's get that left hook working. Keep your guard up and work him onto your left-handers. It's time to take over, Alan.' I could see that these calm but accurate instructions from Jacky were being absorbed as I watched on anxiously and saw the nods from Alan.

Jacky sponged and then dried him, taking the rinsed gum shield from me and placing it in Alan's mouth as the bell sounded for round two.

'Let's go, hands up and get inside,' were the final instructions delivered as Alan headed towards his awaiting opponent.

Jacky joined me again to watch this agonising new experience for me and gave me a wink as we settled in our corner to watch.

I was almost inside the ring now as I edged further along the outside two-foot-wide skirt to make sure I didn't miss anything.

I was feeling pretty helpless but at the same time hopeful, as my younger brother, who certainly wasn't lacking in courage, set about carrying out his mid-round instructions that instantly provided effective changes.

Alan was now moving forward and not allowing his opponent to dictate the fight, sending him round anti-clockwise. He was now scoring, even though he was walking into a few punches to his face but now, once inside, taking full advantage and delivering wicked left hooks to the solar plexus. I could see he was hurting his opponent.

His natural powerful left hook had landed a few times in my stomach during training and only because I was well trained and muscled up was I able to survive these punches. I could imagine what his opponent would be feeling at this time.

'Come on, Alan, more of that,' I was screaming, even though I knew full well he wouldn't hear a single word. Adrenaline would be streaming through his body and he would be oblivious to my shouting, as well as the local crowd noise which was now in full voice. A waste of time, but it definitely made me feel better.

The second round came to an end with Alan on the receiving end of more left jabs; his opponent had analysed Alan's style, I suspected, and reacted. I felt every punch.

Back at our corner I cocked up again as Alan had to wait for the stool for a couple of seconds once I had come to my senses, following one of those looks from Jacky.

During the normal routine of sponging him down, Jacky, in that calming but direct manner, began to provide Alan with instructions for the third and final round. I was ready, this time, with the bucket after Alan had swilled his mouth out.

I knew my younger brother was losing this bout and his only chance of winning would be to stop his opponent. Jacky was obviously of the same opinion and placed a bigger emphasis on getting that left hand into action.

I would probably have thrown caution to the wind and just gone for him if I had been fighting. By contrast, Jacky, calm as ever, continued with the same instructions as round two, adding more emphasis on keeping close inside and working on delivering that left hook to the body.

'Come on, Al,' I mouthed to him with a raised clenched

fist as I handed the gum shield to Jacky in readiness for the last round.

Like the little warrior he was, Alan, without any hesitation, attacked his opponent from the very first second of this final round. Even though he took a couple of good punches on the way in, he let loose with some powerful left-handers that rocked his more talented adversary.

I was more than proud of my young brother; the way he stuck to his guns and the way he was following the mid-round instructions was brilliant. He was working hard and attacking his opponent, albeit taking a few punches to his face. Finally, ducking under an oncoming right cross, Alan delivered a couple of cracking left-handers in quick succession that put his opponent down on one knee.

No stranger to the following protocol, Alan immediately backed over to a neutral corner to await the referee's countdown. I raised a thumb as he looked across, mouthing, 'Great job, well done.'

At the count of seven his opponent rose and the referee immediately grabbed both his hands, going through the motions of cleaning the action parts of his gloves and looking round to make sure Alan was in a neutral corner. It seemed to me like the ref's pitifully slow actions meant he was stalling for time before he finally restarted the fight.

I was now willing Alan to get stuck in, ignore anything coming his way and just attack. I say willing – in reality I was screaming at him to go for it and get it over. Of course, Alan never heard a word, but I couldn't wait for him to continue where he had left off.

The sight of my young brother getting stuck in and doing himself proud had a huge impact on me. As the bout resumed,

Alan set about and attacked a now-recovered adversary who was able to keep him at bay until the bell sounded to end this cracking tournament.

The very appreciative crowd showed their unbiased gratitude after witnessing a great fight with a rousing cheer for both fighters. Even though I hoped I had miscalculated the three rounds' scores, the referee raised Alan's opponent's hand as the result was announced.

I could see the disappointment in my brother's face as he walked back to us. My job then was to convince him that he had done himself proud against a much more experienced boxer. I was feeling his downcast state as he just seemed to clam up and made no comment to either Jacky or me, but he couldn't hide his dissatisfaction.

We walked back towards our changing room with Alan clutching his canteen of cutlery, selected from the prize table in front of the ring. But before reaching the open door, I had to leave him to make it back on his own. Our next club fighter was making his way out of the changing room, heading for the ring.

Much as I wanted to stay by my brother's side, I had work to do. Slapping Alan on the back, I turned and led our next gladiator to the ring.

I was seriously in a daze and just went through the actions with the next two, or even three, fighters without getting excited; all I wanted to do was to make sure my younger brother was OK.

The night finally came to an end with another fantastic overall result for the Phoenix Boxing Club, a resounding night of winners with unfortunately just Alan and one of our heavyweights losing.

This loss certainly had a huge influence on Alan's approach

to training. From then on, he almost mirrored everything I did at the gym, training hard with a new resolve that I had never seen before.

It became a sheer pleasure as, night after night, the Matthews boys set about this boxing game, leaving the rest of our team with mouths open. This new-look regime resulted a couple of months later in Alan fighting for and becoming the Yorkshire Schoolboy champion. I wasn't there, having missed the deadline entry for some reason or other.

During this time, I was becoming more aware of the controversy around boxing being discussed at government level. The future of the sport that I loved was under review and I feared that the end of boxing was imminent.

Why were those so-called influential people trying to boycott boxing? I knew times were changing, memories of the war were beginning to fade and even National Service, where boxing had been widely practised, was said to be coming to an end.

Week after week the papers were full of headlines propagated by Edith Summerskill, a physician and Labour politician from Warrington. She was leading an anti-boxing campaign which even went to a vote in the House of Commons some years later in December 1960.

Against all expectations, it was felt during the next few years that she was winning widespread support. She even suggested, in boxing context, that violence breads violence. Even the Postmaster General (a role abolished in 1969, with responsibilities moving to other roles) was thrown headlong into the debate. From the opposition benches, Summerskill asked, 'Does the Postmaster General think that the frequent displays of boxing tournaments, which glamorises brutality on our television sets, implements fine qualities in our young people?'

An early moral panic in the Fifties that, in my humble opinion, was directed at the young people of my generation. The implication was that we couldn't decide or think for ourselves. Boxing was turning us all into thugs and we were a riot waiting to happen, by all accounts.

I was fuming reading these biased comments. I know that anyone should be able to voice their opinions, but what did they know? How many of these people had ever experienced first-hand what a massive benefit the sport of boxing could provide and had already achieved in the country?

Many people were even starting to believe that boxing in schools and gymnasiums was becoming archaic and, as suggested, a relic of our more violent past. Genghis Khan or Attila the Hun comes to mind.

On the plus side, luckily there were many influential MPs who continually voiced their views about the benefits to the young. Their argument was that boxing 'keeps them fit and off the streets and puts them in the gyms. It keeps them away from flick knives, gangs and away from smoking'.

I would have loved to have been interviewed at that time, to have been given the opportunity to tell it like it really was. Had I been asked my opinions on the virtues of boxing, I would have reiterated the benefits of a sport that had sorted my life out.

Boxing helps youngsters to develop resilience, courage and chivalry. Most importantly it teaches you the ability to control your temper. Young boxers are taught the disciplines of fighting in the ring against an evenly matched opponent –

KO for anti-boxing campaigners

well, mostly – and that whatever skills they are taught in the ring should never be taken out onto the streets.

Wow, I feel better for getting that off my chest. Fortunately, common sense prevailed and the vote to ban boxing was unsuccessful; boxing wouldn't be banned.

*

During my later day running challenges, I often reflected on my early boxing experiences that have frequently been a source of encouragement. Whilst I remember most of my fights, one of the most significant was the 'London Fight', quite a bizarre story which, I believe, needs inclusion.

Three weeks after Alan had fought in Sheffield, I was on my way down to the East End of London for a hastily arranged match that once again meant a lonely midweek train trip.

All the arrangements had been made over the phone and written down for me to follow.

Train tickets and a small brown envelope containing enough cash to keep me from going hungry were waiting for me to collect at the company's social services office, during the afternoon break of my Tuesday day shift.

'Are you happy to take this one on by yourself?' Jacky had asked midway through our training session.

To be honest, I would have travelled to Timbuktu to fight if need be, so yes, I was happy, excited, even, and looking forward to the adventure. London was a magic city that conjured up all sorts of mixed feelings and emotions. At that time in my life, it was like travelling to a different country without needing a passport. Best of all I would also have two shifts off with full pay!

It was time to back off with the heavy training, using this new practice I had started to adopt after listening to Danny's expert advice which had worked a treat during the past couple of fights.

Two weeks before I was due to fight, the taper-down would start, leaving me like a coiled spring waiting to explode on fight day.

The adrenaline had started to flow as I travelled by bus to Doncaster, arriving early with a good hour to wait for the train.

After treating myself to tea and a pack of ginger biscuits, I boarded the train that would take me to our capital city. But as it flew past Rotherham Station, I was nervous that I was sat on the right train!

The lengthy journey gave me time to study my day's itinerary. I read and re-read the written-down instructions of the programme of events for what felt like the next thirty hours or so. I had memorised it to the last detail by the time the train started to slow down leading into the journey's end station.

I was to be met at King's Cross Station by a boxing coach from one of the East End gyms who would look after my needs and welfare for the duration of the tournament.

I had no real idea who I would be fighting later that night. There was not a lot of information to be had on the official enquiry invitation that we had received. We knew that he had held the ABA championship title for the previous year, meaning either he had not retained it or hadn't entered the subsequent national championships. Either way, he must be pretty good, I was thinking when I had accepted the invitation.

As I walked through the exit barrier, I was met by a very

friendly middle-aged bald-headed man named Freddie, who came bounding up towards me, arms waving and shouting my name.

I suppose it wouldn't have taken a lot of detective work to pick out this lone young traveller among the hurrying mature commuters that surrounded me. I probably stood out like a sore thumb as I approached him with my small, brown leather suitcase – well, it was actually Mum's music score case.

We shook hands as he introduced himself in a sort of foreign language – he was obviously a cockney.

Grabbing my case, he turned and led the way, signalling me to follow as we headed for my first trip on the London Underground.

Exciting. Lots of firsts happened that day.

Our conversations were full of 'sorry, I don't understand' or 'could you repeat that, please?' from both of us as we slowly cottoned on to our very different dialects.

Despite the language barrier, I felt very comfortable in Freddie's company. He quickly ran me through the programme of our day and evening together, whilst we travelled along on this fast-moving underground train that was only half full.

A local B&B, close to the boxing venue, had been booked for me. I would be able to relax and rest up for a couple of hours before the fight was due to start later that evening.

'Let's have a bit of nosh, you must hungry, Ray,' Freddie said, standing outside this large cafe just yards before we reached my digs for the night.

There were plenty of meals to choose from, written in white chalk on a large blackboard covering the entire back wall of the cafe. Cod and chips, mushy peas, three slices of bread and butter and a mug of tea seemed like a perfect plan.

I hope you athletes out there are taking note – cod and chips makes for great pre-fight energy food! Only kidding. How very different to the diets of today's modern athletes.

A short walk after devouring my late lunch and I was introduced to the landlady at the B&B, and once again made to feel very welcome.

She was fascinated to learn why I was here, making a comment about me travelling all the way down to the big smoke on my own.

'I know they breed 'em tough up there in Yorkshire,' she said. I was in stitches listening to what they were talking about in cockney slang, for my amusement, I assumed, although half of what was said I didn't have a Scooby-Doo…

As Freddie left me to settle in he said that he'd pick me up around seven, leaving me to scale those steep 'Apples and Pears'. These led to my small, uncarpeted room with a single bed set out under the window. Home for the night.

I was ready and waiting downstairs as my new friend arrived just before seven. It was only a ten-minute walk to the hall, he shouted, as we set off in the opposite direction from the cafe into the noisy traffic-filled road, zig-zagging through the crowds.

With coat collar pulled up and head down to stave off the drizzle that had been slowly coming down most of the late afternoon, we crossed over this busy road and jogged most of the way to the venue.

Good as his word, ten minutes later we entered the hall that was staging the fights. Freddie, a local celebrity, it seemed, by the way he was greeted, introduced me to the fight promoter, who thanked me for coming at such short notice. He made a bit of a fuss as I was further introduced to the main sponsor of the night's fights.

'We have reserved a gold watch as your prize tonight if you should win,' emphasising the big '*if*'. Was this guy trying to scare me? Bad move, I thought, as we were directed across the hall to my allocated changing room.

My opponent was ushered in as the pre-fight protocol got underway. The weigh-in gave me a first sighting of his physique. About an inch taller than me with well-muscled arms and broad shoulders but really skinny legs that didn't look strong enough to hold him up.

There were just a few ounces in it at the weigh-in, in my favour for a change. We then waited together for the doctor's inspection, without any comment from either of us as we sized each other up.

I can never understand why, once the doctor has got a handful of your 'Christmas crackers', does he ask you to cough? Believe me, you actually do get used to that last bit of the medical.

I was in the zone now, raring to go, and couldn't wait to get the fight underway.

8

Following in Ivanhoe's footsteps

You know how it is: you wake up in the morning, yawn, have a good stretch and before you swing those legs out of bed, you ask yourself that question, 'Do I really want to run another marathon?'

Funnily enough, I always seemed to come up with the same old answer – 'You bet I do!' And off I went to run another marathon, just a normal day at the office.

How divergent it was starting to feel; a new sense of duty to begin with, but then, day after day, a sense of pride that I was, against all expected probabilities, actually enjoying every one of these marathons, clocking up the miles that my body was admirably coping with.

A good night's sleep, crucial to the success of this challenge, often depended on a short post-marathon evening trip up the motorway to Hoyland and the clinic of Pure Physiotherapy where Team Kay would be waiting, often with her daughters, Emily and Alice, to untie a knot or two.

There had been an anxious spell, about a quarter of the way into the challenge, where the old hamstrings were really playing up, generally kicking in after around eight miles or so into the day's marathon. I would make the call, usually mid-afternoon, and could just imagine Kay's face when my name popped up on her mobile screen, anxiously wondering, 'Now what's he done?'

After the early evening's session with Kay, I would travel home back down the M1, confident that I would be fit and ready for the following day's marathon. This secure feeling would be the perfect medicine to lull me off to sleep, like a tranquilliser that removes any sense of doubt. Who needs pills?

As I ramped up the miles, the pre-marathon training had physically prepared me well for the challenge. But nothing could prepare me for one of the most bizarre incidents of my entire life that occurred during one of those morning training sessions.

I vividly remember the day. It was a Sunday and, having set off early morning, I was expecting to complete the run, around twenty miles, and be back home in time for dinner.

Having completed most of the miles, I was on my way back home after skirting around Roche Abbey feeling good.

The sun was shining, it was a glorious day and all I was wearing was a pair of shorts and, of course, my trusty New Balance 860 shoes that I was alternating as instructed, which were performing well.

With the old vitamin D on my body, I was feeling great and running well. Having just completed the last of the climbs on the lower Maltby Crags path, in auto-pilot mode without a care in the world, I heard this cry for help.

'Help, can you help? Have you got a phone, mister?'

I stopped and looked up to where this plea was coming

from and I could see a young woman with two small children halfway up the hillside.

'Sorry,' I shouted back with outstretched arms, wondering where she would think I could carry a phone but at the same time looking up to where she was pointing.

'Blinking 'eck,' I gulped.

I could see this middle-aged man perched on a branch in a mid-sized tree on the side of the hill above her.

'Oh my God! He's got a rope around his neck,' I muttered to myself out loud.

I scrambled off the path up the steep bank side and ran towards this chilling vision above me, at the same time looking up and trying to evaluate the actual situation that I was heading towards – and what I could do to help.

On closer inspection, I could see that the rope was tied off on a branch around four or five feet above him. This was a serious and traumatic sight to say the least and one that threw me into a bit of a wobble.

This only happens in films, doesn't it?

'Don't panic, Ray, stay calm. Surely I can talk him down,' I was thinking.

I politely suggested that the woman take her young kids away from the scene. I was worried for their welfare. They'd be scarred for life if they were to witness what I expect we both presumed was coming next. Besides, one of us needed to find a phone to call for help.

I turned back to talk to the guy perched on a branch fifteen feet above me, as the young woman and her two children headed up the hillside.

The guy, who looked around fifty years old, unshaven and sort of unkempt, was motionless and just staring into space.

'What's your name, mate?' I managed to get out from a very dry, tight mouth. 'Are you from Maltby?' I asked, wishing I knew more about how to deal with the situation.

'Is there anyone I could bring to help?' I asked. Still no response and not even any sign that I was getting through to him.

I calmly talked to him for the next quarter of an hour or so, which seemed like at least an hour, without any reply or comment whatsoever as I continued in my attempts at trying to coax him down.

I couldn't tell if the variety of topics that I talked about was working for him, or even getting through – it was certainly helping me to calm down, though, if nothing else. Above all, I was hoping and praying that someone with a greater knowledge of these sort of things would suddenly appear and take over.

Isn't it just typical, when you desperately need help there's never anyone around? Obviously, I realised, that at around two o'clock on a Sunday afternoon, every Tom, Dick and Harry would be at home having a roast dinner, like I should be.

As time passed, I was beginning to feel more confident that help would be on its way and he was probably not going to jump now, even though his zombie-like facial expressions had never altered since I arrived. Keep talking, Ray!

'Let me help you down, mate,' I suggested, as nothing else seemed to be getting through.

Then all of a sudden, without any warning, he started to move, screaming expletives, and jumped.

He dropped like a stone, bouncing back like a concertina as the rope came under tension.

I was in shock. It took a few seconds to register that he

had actually jumped and his feet were dangling just over two or three foot above me.

With no other option left, jumping into action I scrambled up the tree to get to where the rope was fastened on the branch above. Fortunately, there were plenty of staggered branches which made my task almost as easy as climbing a ladder.

My fingers worked desperately to loosen the knot, but try as I might I knew it would be impossible to undo the rope without taking the weight off the knot.

Whenever I think about this traumatic incident, I always ask myself that same question: where does that extra strength when needed in circumstances like this come from? Somehow, all of a sudden I was able to get enough grip and leverage on the rope below the branch, finding the strength to lift him high enough to take the pressure off the rope, so I could untie the double knot.

Oh hell, it was taking ages! Don't panic, Ray. He had made a pretty good job of the knot.

The narrow branch five foot above on which I was precariously balancing was beginning to move, because I had all his weight and he was now shaking violently, dragging me forward. Unable to steady myself, I was left with no option but to let go, after trying to feed the rope through my hands to steadily lower him to the ground.

He crashed to the ground below, snapping a lower branch on the way down.

As I looked down from above him, I could see that he was lying unconscious in a heap with what looked like a broken leg, which was pointing out at an unnatural angle.

What a relief, as my eyes followed the sound that was being made above the tree line at the top of the crags.

Me at twelve years old, May 1953

Alan at the beginning of his boxing around 1954/55

Part supply of New Balance running shoes. Following me everywhere…

Running at the end of the Brinsworth 10K during the second marathon. Photo thanks to Alex Roebuck

Some of the Brits heading off to France

My last wave goodbye

One of the loops during the second day's marathons along the canal

Adam looking better than expected at around twenty-mile mark

Soaking wet but still full of running

My impressive escort and friends on the final run into Newman School

The final few feet crossing the finish line, bringing an end to the running part of the challenge

Posing for photos with the children, parents and staff

Thank you for the amazing reception at the end of the seventy-five marathons

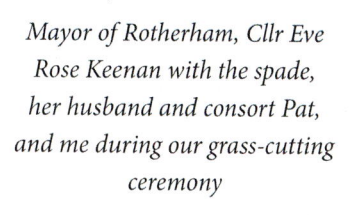

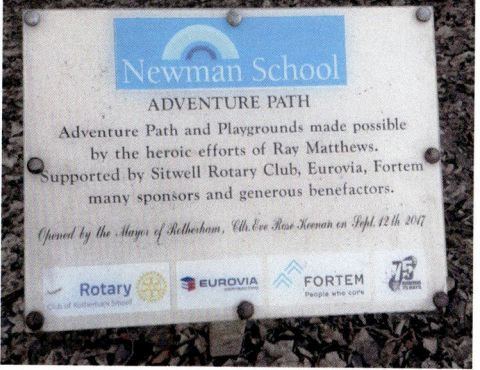

Above: The management team, Paul Sylvester, Eve Rose Keenan and her consort husband Pat and me ready to get the path underway

Mayor of Rotherham, Cllr Eve Rose Keenan with the spade, her husband and consort Pat, and me during our grass-cutting ceremony

The commemorative plaque, erected at the side of the lower playground. It even shows my marathon logo in the bottom right corner

My first fundraising meeting with the Newman School Children

Me with a group of Newman School children. Dominic, Sean and Mick

A leisurely saunter on the new path

First walk on the meandering path through the woods

Left: Holly, looking every bit the part, and in big demand on the Red Carpet at the Pride of Britain Award ceremony

Below: Adam Fowler presenting me with the Pride of Britain Award with Paul Sylvester looking on

British Citizen Award medal presentation.
Courtesy of British Citizen Awards

*Maureen with
one of the Palace Guards*

I could see the tell-tale green overalled paramedic coming over the hill down one of the well-trodden paths towards us, whilst I descended the tree. He arrived almost as I set foot on solid ground.

The paramedic threw off his rucksack and quickly jumped into action, establishing that his new patient was breathing.

The feeling of helplessness was soon replaced with joy as I saw a thumbs-up sign from the paramedic.

I heaved a great sigh of relief, realising that, fearing the worst, I had been holding my breath in anticipation, and somewhat thankful that I wasn't the one who would have been responsible for attempting resuscitation.

I already felt a sense of responsibility for letting him go and possibly causing even more damage than if I could have gently lowered him down. On reflection, I realised that it was impossible to hold on any longer without me following him down, from an even greater height, and probably headbutting the ground.

An ambulance must have arrived a few minutes later on Blyth Road above the Crags and, within no time at all, two more of the medical team, one carrying a stretcher, the other with a small rucksack on his back, came scrambling down the hill towards us.

The mother and her two children, who must have been waiting on the roadside to give directions for the blue-lit ambulance as they arrived, had followed the ambulance personnel down to this poor guy who was still laying limp and hadn't moved since hitting the deck.

The youngest boy looked up to me and asked, 'Is he dead, mister?'

I shuddered.

After further investigations, now safely in the hands of these specialists, the guy was finally declared fit to be moved, and believe me, it's a hell of a hill climb over the Crags up to the waiting ambulance on the main road above. Between them, however, they managed to stretcher the now-conscious guy, who still hadn't uttered a word, up to the ambulance.

I was in a bit of a mess, to be honest, and sweating cobs once the realisation and the enormity of this incident finally hit home.

Had I handled the situation correctly? Had I talked to him using the right words? And, worst of all, would he have jumped if I had not been there? All questions to which I would never receive an answer. The only consolation was that he was still alive.

I can't even imagine how low and desperate you have to get to want to take your own life. But worse still, how serious and complex it must be when you actually go through the motions, intending to end it all.

I understand suicide is a national social issue, particularly prevalent in men under fifty years of age. In Rotherham, the rate of suicide deaths is higher than the national average. Not good at all.

But we are all very different from one another and can count ourselves fortunate that most of us will never be driven to these extremes. This experience really brought home how lucky I am to have gone through life without ever experiencing suicidal thoughts.

There's much to be said about exercise and its benefits on both physical and mental health.

If you have or are experiencing any form of mental ill health, please don't bottle it up inside. It's OK not to be

OK. Talking to your family, friends or an impartial person or support service can help others understand how you are feeling.

I set off for home at speed, arriving to an expected, 'Where have you been? Your dinner's been ready for a while,' from Maureen. I was forgiven once I explained my delay at getting home.

The roast lamb dinner helped to ease the situation. I even treated myself to a cool pint of Foster's!

Later that evening I rang the hospital trying to find out how he was.

'Are you a relation?' I was asked by someone on the end of the phone at Rotherham Hospital. 'Then sorry, I am not allowed to give out that information.' The explanation of who I was didn't make a blind bit of difference.

As it happens, a nurse friend of mine rang later to let me know that he was OK, no broken leg, and had actually been discharged that same day and taken home by his daughter. To this day, I still have no idea who he is or how his life is.

I have run countless times along that same path and always have thoughts about his welfare whenever I pass that tree.

I just had to be there, at that time, on that day, as memories of the traumatic experience come flooding back.

There's a lot to be said for Sunday morning marathon training.

*

Time to get back to our daily bread.

It's always a great pleasure to run alongside like-minded

athletes and I had been looking forward to an incredible weekend of running with two brilliant local clubs.

On Saturday 30th July, the twenty-ninth marathon, organised by Pat Rooney from the Kimberworth Striders, encompassed a route that would be partially run along the Trans-Pennine Trail (TPT).

Earlier that morning, I had already completed ten miles around Firbeck village and Laughton-en-le-Morthen before I arrived at the arranged car park midway alongside the trail path.

What a great reception from the enthusiastic twenty-five or so Striders, as well as Hope the Border collie with her owner Helen, a long-standing friend who joined her running mates to make the marathon a memorable one.

We set off as a group, turning back 360-degrees onto the TPT before running as far as Meadowhall Shopping Centre. The flat tree-lined route along the trail formed part of a very pleasant loop before returning back along Grange Mill Lane to where we had started from. As flat a route you could find anywhere in and around Rotherham, thanks Pat.

Evidence of distance markers were lined off along the level tarmac path, indicating that this was a much-used speed training path by the Striders.

The twenty-ninth marathon ended for me around 2:30pm with a large group photo in the bright sunshine, as we completed the long climb up Droppingwell Lane, finishing in the car park at the entrance to Millmoor Juniors Football Club grounds.

A big shout-out to Mr Peter Lounds for the vast number of photographs of various groups of runners around the course, and also the £75 pledged donation. He had enough faith that I would complete the seventy-five marathons and had been saving a pound every day of the challenge. Once again, thank you, you're a star.

After a very pleasant morning of running and another marathon dusted off, I said my thanks and goodbyes amid rousing cheers from the runners of Kimberworth Striders. I then high-tailed it home to get some sleep in readiness for a further marathon later that day – or maybe that should be early the next morning. Whichever way you look at it, it wasn't going to be long before I was running another marathon.

I had made arrangements to complete the thirtieth marathon using the 'Dusk Till Dawn' off-road trail race organised by the runners of the Manvers Waterfront Boat Club and runners.

This event is exactly what it says on the tin. It's an off-road running event that starts at six in the evening and continues around a 3.21-mile loop of a now-mature man-made lake near Wath-upon-Dearne, coming to a conclusion at six o'clock the following morning.

The idea of this unique running event is to run as far or as little as you want in those twelve hours. This fitted in, I was just about to say nicely, but let's just say it fitted in with my marathon challenge.

I did manage to get a couple of hours sleep during Saturday afternoon and, after refuelling with my supplement and weighing myself, not forgetting to log the results, I set off for Manvers, arriving around 5:30pm.

The majority of the entrants, most of whom were friends and running colleagues, were aware of my challenge and made it clear that they were impressed with my achievements to date.

Photo sessions with groups and individual selfies were requested, together with promises of donations to come. This made it all worthwhile as we prepared to head from the clubhouse to the start line, in the car park behind the boat shed, and get the race underway.

We set off as the clock moved round to 6pm and, as with any normal race, the fast guys and gals were away like rabbits into the evening sun, quickly disappearing out of view. The rest of us mere mortals, mostly still in conversation, settled into our slower pace.

I was well prepared and already dressed for the cool night air to come, perfect for steady plodding lap after lap, and being passed every three laps or so by the eventual winner.

As the night drew in it became pitch black and very cool along the tree-lined avenue down the northern side of the lake.

With my trusty Petzle LED head torch now activated, a clear path was being illuminated, making it possible to clearly see the lumps and bumps on the way ahead. The light cut through the darkness around the lake, especially when two or three athletes came together as a group; it looked more like Blackpool illuminations.

This is a great and unique event where every athlete taking part has the opportunity to push themselves into achieving a PB or whatever they choose to get out of the event within the twelve hours of running time available.

The organisers also offered a quiet room within the clubhouse where athletes could have a short rest, or even sleep for a while, before continuing.

Ample food and drink, served by willing club members and colleagues, were constantly available at the end of every lap, making this overnight event a runner's dream, pardon the pun.

A coloured rubber wrist band would be placed on your wrist at the end of each lap, which was used to establish the end results of every athlete by simply multiplying the number of bands by the 3.21 miles per lap which would provide the overall distance. Uncomplicated and pretty accurate. The fast guys ended up with an armful of these coloured rubber bands before the 6am cut-off.

Most of the athletes were aiming for distances that they had never attempted before. With twelve hours to go at, there were many PBs throughout the event, with athletes producing beyond their expectations, creating a huge sense of achievement from this very different concept to a normal race event.

Running through the night, probably using head torches for the very first time as well, added to the challenge that most of the athletes sadistically enjoyed.

My intention was to run a good part of this thirtieth marathon into Sunday morning, in keeping with a marathon a day for seventy-five days.

I eventually finished at around 3:30am. Overall, I'd run a grand total of nine laps of the lake, resulting in a display of 28.75 miles on my Garmin watch. Almost half of these miles were ran post-midnight.

I was more than happy with the pretty accurate workings that my watch displayed, which once again proved that the distance I was achieving every day provided factual evidence between calculated and actual distances shown on my watch.

After clocking up the (just over) marathon distance, I decided to stay for a while, helping the athletes who were still out running where I could, until the first lights of dawn arrived around 5am.

It was finally time to head for home, content that I had survived and had completed another marathon, albeit in complete contrast to my usual daylight environments.

Other than feeling sleepy I was in great spirits, with no aches or pains, and best of all, I had the full day ahead of me without running. A whole new experience as I would be able to enjoy spending some time during the day with Maureen – the first time in over a month.

Happy and content, I headed for bed and slept soundly for a few hours until midday before chilling out in the sunshine until it was time to write up my reports for Kay and Barry.

For the following day's marathon, I had planned to run part of the old Northern Triangle event. This route would take me close to Doncaster with part of the run on the riverbank down into Sprotbrough and beyond.

The Doncaster Doddle, the Darlington Dash and the Round Rotherham, aptly named the Northern Triangle challenge, consisted of a thirty-, a forty- and then a fifty-mile off-road event that was completed over three weekends. But sadly only the fifty-mile Round Rotherham event remains.

*

'Morning, Ray. How are you today and where are we up to now with the marathon count?' asked Rony Robinson from BBC Radio Sheffield. Our usual Monday morning chat was a little earlier this week, at just before 10am. I had been contacted a few minutes earlier as I approached Conisbrough and was looking forward to our weekly chat.

'Morning, Rony, we are on our thirty-first marathon today and I am looking up at Conisbrough Castle. I have never been inside this castle, so after we have spoken, I will be using my old-age privilege and hopefully get a cheap senior citizens' pass to have a quick look round.'

It had taken me the best part of an hour from starting at 9am, running across to Conisbrough over the fields and down through the village of Braithwell, across to Clifton village and skirting around Crookhill Park golf course on the outskirts of Edlington, down into the low road, which leads up to Castle Hill and the main entrance to the castle.

'I am stood in the small garden area of Coronation Park which wraps around the World War I memorial below the castle. I'm now looking up at the statue of an infantryman stood with his rifle and fixed bayonet. There are also a dozen or so poppy wreaths from the last Armistice Day scattered around the base which are still looking relatively fresh,' I told Rony and the radio listeners.

'I can't believe you're still going strong. Everyone tells me it's impossible what you're doing day after day, but you're proving them all wrong. Good on ya, Ray,' Rony said.

'So, how's your bum then?' he suddenly asked.

We hadn't talked about nipples for a couple of weeks, so I suppose I shouldn't have been surprised at the new controversial topic he had opened up with.

It looked as though my derrière was on the menu this week.

I reckoned he'd been talking to a runner again who had experienced excruciating pain from chapped buttocks which develops from sweating and friction, generally from running distances over at least a half marathon. Pretty much like 'nipple rash' that we had comprehensively covered earlier.

'So far so good, Rony, but it does remind me of a very funny true story about Mick, one of my running mates, myself and a jar of Vaseline.'

'Do tell, Ray,' he requested.

He once again caught me by surprise, half expecting him to have talked over that comment and taken us down a different but relatively safe avenue of conversation. But this was Rony Robinson I was talking to, after all, don't forget, and, other than foul language being barred on live radio, almost nothing else was off-limits.

The story goes that Mick and I were stood in the holding zones with the rest of the runners overlooking the city during the start of one of my Edinburgh marathons. I remember it was a freezing cold morning, we were dressed to kill, adorned in black bin liner plastic bags, shielding us from the bitterly westerly wind. We began to prepare, like you do, going through the ritual of lubricating all the parts of skin that could rub together over the length of a marathon, which includes applying oodles of Vaseline under armpits, nipples and also between the cheeks of your bum.

'Once bitten, twice shy, eh, Rony?' I laughed. 'But there's a certain unwritten protocol that's to be observed between running buddies, Rony, especially if you're sharing your mate's tub of Vaseline.'

Of this I was serious, as I had learnt all those years ago.

If you think about it it's only fair that you dip your finger into his jar only *once* when you're applying lubrication to your nether regions. But guess who needed a second helping, and guess what Mick's comment was as I tried to prod the same finger that I had used the first time into Mick's tub of Vaseline?

Well, here's a clue, it ended in off!

Mick quickly withdrew the tub from my reach and gave me a very stern look, shaking his head in disgust.

I could hear the choked laughter from Rony as he quickly digested the story I was telling him.

We talked further about how I was feeling and coping with the day-to-day marathons and where our fundraising had reached. We concluded our morning light-hearted conversation with a promise from Rony to keep mentioning our Golden Giving site and fundraising goal as the music faded, signalling the end of that week's live radio link.

I bade farewell to Rony and jogged up Castle Hill to the castle entrance, which looked fairly new but had been constructed in a sympathetic manner by skilled craftsmen to blend well with the medieval castle walls.

I entered through the open door, walking towards the reception desk, and was greeted like a long-lost cousin by one of the young attendants.

'No charge, Mr Matthews,' she said.

I looked at this young woman in front of me inquisitively. 'How do you know my name?' I asked.

'You've just given the castle more publicity in half an hour than we have had in years,' she said. 'We have just been listening to your live interview on Radio Sheffield. Very funny,' she added.

They had actually been waiting for me to arrive.

How good is this running marathons malarkey? I know it's not supposed to be fun, but it's a guilty pleasure I was experiencing day after day, while most people thought I was having a tough time of it. Well, now you know the truth.

Conisbrough Castle was built in the eleventh century, commissioned by William de Warenne, 1st Earl of Surrey, after the Norman Conquest in 1066 (I remember this date from my school days). This imposing structure dominates the skyline with its ninety-seven-foot high keep, which can be seen for miles around, one of the best surviving examples of defensive architecture in South Yorkshire.

I entered the castle via a grassy bank and lawned area, which I suspect is used for picnics and games during festival weeks. I proceeded through the entrance to the castle and stepped onto the re-instated floors which allowed access to many parts of this English Heritage-managed castle.

I have a thing about climbing. If I see a hill, I just have to run up it. In this case, the spiral staircase drew me like a magnet and before I knew it I was stood on top of the keep looking out at the surrounding countryside far beyond Conisbrough.

After half an hour of working my way down, visiting various interesting rooms, it was time to make tracks and say farewell to my new followers on the way out.

There is much to be said about this old castle which inspired Sir Walter Scott enough to write about the legendary Ivanhoe. But it was time for this other old relic to leave and head off towards River Don to pick up the Trans-Pennine Trail and carry on the day's marathon.

After crossing the viaduct to the far side of the River Don, I headed south down the wide footpath along the river into Sprotbrough, the childhood home of World War II flying ace Douglas Bader. Here I could take advantage of the nice weather and enjoy my blackcurrant jam sandwiches on one of the benches along the riverside.

Enjoying a pleasant interlude, I sat with my back comfortably settled on a nearby bench watching the canal wildlife activities. This gave me time to reflect on the one thing that was mostly in my mind of late – fundraising, or the lack of it, to be precise. The stream of donations had diluted down to a trickle, which was, in general, the only cause for concern in an otherwise perfect challenge.

How could we give the fundraising a boost after listening to people telling me that this extreme challenge ought to be raking in thousands of pounds? It was frustrating to say the least, so what did I need to do to make that sort of cash injection happen?

A short phone call soon had me smiling again. I was talking to Nicola from BBC Look North, again, as she came up with one of her brilliant ideas that she had mentioned at the end of our last filming session.

'What about a visit to your doctor whilst filming you running around Maltby? And then we could do some filming whilst you're having a treatment session with your physio,' she suggested.

It was like she had the perfect answer to my plea for help. TV coverage would almost certainly give our fundraising a kick up the backside and provide the almost guaranteed boost it so badly needed.

I told Nicola I'd need to clear it with my GP, Dr Khan and my physio Kay, but would get back to her with suggested dates and times.

With a spring in my step, I headed on down the river at an invigorated jog on the well-trodden path towards Hexthorpe, feeling happy and content, safe in the knowledge that TV coverage would give our fundraising a major boost, before turning west to complete the last thirteen or so miles for home.

*

Guest contributions from some of my fellow runners

Helen Doyle

I remember saying that we probably wouldn't be seeing Helen again, as she struggled during her first training run with our group of newish runners. But how wrong was I? Made of true Yorkshire grit, we went on to share many races together around South Yorkshire and, most notably of all, the Edinburgh Marathon, followed by successfully completing the fifty-mile Rowbotham's Round Rotherham. Helen is a valued family friend.

Ray Matthews

I have been friends with Ray now for many years. It was he who introduced me to running and we have shared many miles together.

Leading up to Ray's seventy-fifth birthday he told me about his plan to run seventy-five marathons in seventy-five days. Most people would laugh at this point and call him crazy. I, however, had no doubt that Ray would complete every step of those marathons and so I just asked when and how he would be doing them.

He asked for each marathon to be sponsored by local businesses with the proceeds raised to be given to Newman School in Rotherham.

At the time I was working for a Yorkshire firm of solicitors called Switalskis, who kindly offered to host one of the marathon days from their Pontefract office.

On the day of this marathon Ray joined a team of runners from the law firm, me included, and we set out to Pontefract racecourse, looped around the course and back through the local sites of Pontefract, circling back to the office before leaving Ray to complete his adventure.

Ray never ceases to amaze me; he has always dreamed big with his running goals and always delivers.

A few years ago, Ray wrote a book called *Me and My Shadow*. Now, you can't always see your shadow, but you always know it is there with you by your side walking your path. Ray's wonderful wife Maureen is always by his side supporting his goals.

Ray has inspired people of all ages and abilities along his way, sharing his journey with others and encouraging people to start their own.

Here is wishing you a happy eightieth birthday, Ray, and to the next adventure that awaits you…

*

Sharon Tait

Sharon took up running after a serious injury. To achieve what she has, including completing the Jane Tomlinson 10k over a challenging course in York, demonstrates the character that she possesses. I am also gratified that she took my advice!

Ray Matthews

I have enjoyed running for a number of years, being introduced to it by my physiotherapist. I had tried many different exercise regimes to no avail and found it difficult to motivate myself due to mental health issues and pain.

My physio told me to just gently start walking and running and gradually build up and see if that helped with my physical and mental wellbeing. It was hard work, but I was determined to get my life back together, and gradually my fitness increased and my mood became more positive.

If only my doctor had prescribed running instead of handing out anti-depressants!

Fast forward ten years and I was working at Switalskis Solicitors when it was decided the law firm would sponsor Ray for his thirty-fourth marathon.

Ray had completed the first half of the marathon before we joined him at our office in Ropergate, heading out along Park Road into Pontefract Racecourse then back to the office, continuing this loop until we had completed the second half of the marathon.

I was nervous as I had never really run that sort of distance before, usually sticking to 10km. My colleagues Steve, Sarah and Helen along with Ray were all seasoned marathon runners and then there was me!

There was no need to worry. We all settled into a steady pace together and I ran alongside Ray to find out first-hand about his motivation and mental attitude to be able to achieve so much. Ray's advice and positivity have stuck with me to this day. We discussed hill-running and how best to prepare your body for running long distances.

Sarah and Helen had to break off from this challenge as they had to get back to the office. By mile twelve, my body was starting to tire so I told Steve and Ray to leave me and I would walk back. Being true gentlemen, they wouldn't hear of it and started to walk with me so that I could have some recovery time.

We headed back towards the office, running again by this time, and headed for the tree-lined Valley Gardens to finish off our morning's run with Ray. A perfect place to finish Ray's marathon with Team Switalskis – the longest run of my life.

I left Ray to eat his pie and peas in our office – I think he deserved it!

*

Ian Hopper

I first met Ian ten years ago and, with similar interests and values, we gelled then and have ever since. I was delighted that he was able to join me on the sixty-seventh marathon, a truly memorable day. You meet some fantastic people when running. Ian is one of them.

Ray Matthews

I first met Ray at the start area of the Venice Marathon in 2011; there weren't many people in deepest Italy wearing a running vest from South Yorkshire! We got on chatting and, after completing a highly enjoyable and atmospheric marathon, we have kept in touch ever since. As soon as I found out he was planning to do seventy-five marathons on consecutive days after his seventy-fifth birthday, I just had to join him for one of them.

The day spent running with Ray in South Yorkshire on marathon day number sixty-seven was absolutely magical. It was a sunny day, with great company and very enjoyable 'towpath' running – we even had time for cups of tea and cake at regular intervals as well!

Ray is undoubtedly a real local personality and it was great to see how many folk wanted to stop for a chat and a catch-up – happy days!

Running a marathon is a serious undertaking; the training, preparation and mental toughness required is considerable. To complete a marathon is a real achievement, but to do seventy-five after your seventy-fifth birthday is absolutely staggering. Ray's achievement is both incredible and inspirational and it was a delight to be with him on one of those journeys.

9

Introduction to boxing's dark side

Back to the London story. The uneventful lengthy train journey into King's Cross Station had provided me with the time to think, time to reflect and take stock on my six-year career. Thus far, it had provided me with the sort of apprenticeship that few of my opponents would ever experience. I had, at the same time, been taught the values and principles that would continue to be the backbone of my life and uphold right up to this present time of my life.

Safely booked into a small and very friendly B&B that would be home for the night, somewhere to sleep and have breakfast before heading off for home tomorrow, the rest of the afternoon was free for me to rest up and chill out until it was time for my new best friend to pick me up for the fight.

Freddie arrived just before seven, sauntering into the small reception room of this old Victorian terraced three-storey house and, after a couple of minutes of explanations of how the night would pan out, we set off for the venue.

We made it to the fight venue without getting soaked and with time to kill before the proceedings would begin.

I was having a nosey around the already packed hall that appeared much larger than the outside indicated when Freddie suddenly appeared from one of the doors next to my changing room and introduced me to my new second for the night, a tough-looking six-footer who looked as though one of those big red London double-decker buses had run over his face. An ex-pro who still had his heart and soul in the game, I reckoned as he came towards me.

Freddie would be looking after my needs together with this giant of a man, who, after I had been introduced to him, shadowed me everywhere I went like a minder.

Sorry, I can't remember his name, but Sam seems to fit the bill. Sam it is then.

Shaking an outstretched hand, I feared the worst and was ready to pull my hand away from an expected crushing from his size nine shovel-like paw. Fortunately, to my relief, Sam had a relatively gentle grip as we introduced ourselves.

We then headed off to the far corner of the building and were soon settled into our part of the shared changing room to prepare for the fight.

Weigh-in and doctor's inspection all OK, and for once in a long while, I was the heavier of the two of us, but only by a couple of ounces.

My opponent, who was a good inch taller than me, had the body of an athlete but the legs of a chicken. Unusually skinny to say the least.

Even though I was a professional at taping up other fighter's hands before a fight, it's difficult to get the right tension when taping up your own. I would never have made an acceptable job of it myself as it's a work of art to get it spot on. However, my new friend Sam, who genuinely seemed to be on my side, made a better job of it than even Jacky had managed before.

My hands felt good and strong, but as there was almost three quarters of an hour to kill before it was fight time, there was no reason to put the gloves on until just before it was time to head out to the ring.

'Never judge a book by its cover,' I thought of Sam as we sat facing one another, while he expertly bandaged up my hands and we talked comfortably together as though we had known each other for years.

Sam, who, despite displaying all the scars and damage that years of tough fighting had planted on his face, was so very calm and quietly spoken. He, as I quickly learned, possessed a mass of knowledge that transcended way beyond anything I thought I knew or had read about. His gentle demeanour was also actually helping to calm the nerves that had kicked in as the clock ticked ever closer to fight time.

He had been a professional boxer for over twenty years, learning his trade in the back streets of London, and had fought all over the globe. Having been a bare-knuckle fighter in the States, the illegal booths in London, Sam had also spent some time, after weeks of sea travel, bare-knuckle fighting in Australia; I was just mesmerised.

Sam had this air of zen about him, as he calmly made sure I was ready to perform. With hands the size of shovels to aim at, I spent a few minutes loosening off, gently punching at the large targets.

I was in good hands, pardon the pun. I felt so comfortable and relaxed with my new makeshift away team, as the fight time drew nearer the adrenaline started to kick in.

I had a job to do. I was ready and time was closing in.

Freddie appeared at the door and, after a thumbs-up sign, we made our way down between the avenue of seated supporters to the massive ring in the centre of this Tardis of a hall.

We climbed the four wooden steps up into the red, white and blue-coloured four-roped ring, which displayed the promoters' logos pattern in the centre of the canvas and four corner post bags, and stepped into the ring.

Less than thirty seconds later, as I stood in my corner, coating the bottom of my boots in the resin tray, two hundred or more partisan supporters gave my opponent a loud, boisterous cheer whilst I waited for him to enter the ring. The noise was deafening. I got the feeling that he had entertained this crowd on many occasions.

'So, I will be fighting the crowd as well tonight,' I thought, as I had only received a subdued amount of applause from the home crowd. Very partisan, but I was used to that. It's like adding coal to the fire!

But then came the MC's announcement, the like of which I had never experienced before, after my opponent had entered the ring. Total showbiz-style with all the razzamatazz of a World Championship bout, following the build-up of stirring music.

Then, as was becoming the norm, he announced that I was there all the way from Sheffield, Yorkshire.

'Doesn't Rotherham exist on any map?' I wanted to shout and put him right.

But the MC was in full swing now and the time it took for him to announce 'Raaaaaaaaaay Matthews' seemed longer to reel off than it takes to say, 'I am here all the way from Rotherham tonight to take the trophy away from your boy.'

I was now fired up and ready to go, the nerves settled and under control.

Our immaculately dressed referee for the evening, an ex-fighter, easily recognisable by the busted nose and cauliflower ear, and a Cockney to boot, had brought us together in the middle of the ring to deliver his well-rehearsed instructions to us both. As his instructions concluded, we made our way back to our respective corners ready for the first round.

Adrenaline was surging through my body. I took a deep breath and slowly exhaled, as I looked across at my opponent waiting for the bell to get the bout underway.

He was feeling the tension, I could tell by the look in his eyes and the twitch he had suddenly developed around his face. Freddie gently massaged the muscles across the top of my shoulders as I waited.

The bell sounded loud in my ears, which triggered the plan I had been forming for a while into action.

I floated across the large ring, meeting him well before he had time to reach halfway, and hit him full in the face with a solid right-hander. He half dropped towards the canvas but managed to control his descent as he ended up balancing on one knee in his own corner, with the referee shielding him from any further punching from me.

He wasn't badly hurt, probably more shocked than damaged. I had missed the target; the punch landed well above his jaw without a great deal of solid power. Nevertheless, I was pleased that the unconventional start had worked and would unsettle my opponent for the rest of the fight.

How many amateur boxers would ever deliver a right cross without sending a straight left beforehand? That's how we were taught to box. We were originally instructed using a series of patterns that make up the basics and forms the way almost every amateur performs. Jabs almost inevitably start the moves.

The hours of sparring with Danny had taught me that I would have to learn to become unpredictable if I were to progress.

The count was slow and deliberate, but my opponent was fully conscious as he hung on to the corner ropes. I had no doubt that he would have been totally surprised with my unorthodox start. He had been on the receiving end of a sucker punch that I had planned to start the fight off with.

I had remembered the opening punch that had KO'd Bruce Woodcock from Doncaster at the start of his unsuccessful world title fight in America a few years before. I had been listening to the radio, having got up at five in the morning, and was so disappointed when, within a few seconds of the first-round bell sounding, Bruce was on the deck out for the count.

Back to my fight and Freddie was giving me a thumbs-up sign as I looked across to my corner.

My opponent had been given the compulsory count as well as the mandatory glove wipe down on the immaculate white shirt of the referee.

At the signal to fight, wide-eyed and now very wary, my opponent moved swiftly around the ring, back-pedalling to stay out of reach, giving himself time to settle. That wasn't in my plans, though, as I stalked him, delivering punch after punch. I attacked once again, driving him into his corner under this barrage of punches.

His covering was pretty secure as he crouched in front of me. But there's always gaps which can be opened up. I set

Introduction to boxing's dark side

about hammering him around his ribs, but I wasn't ready for what came next. I was grabbed, literally lifted off my feet and spun round into his corner.

I was suddenly being mauled, his head rubbing across my face, a thumb in my eye and a sharp elbow right across my cheek bone.

My immediate reaction was to lash out and land anything that would connect, unknowing what was best to do under this extreme dirty fouling.

Surely the referee could see what had just happened. Why wasn't he intervening? It left me with no option but to push out, lash out and get away from where I was trapped. But the persistent rubbing from his gloves was already smarting my left eye, making it difficult to see where I could get to safety.

This baptism of fire sparked a sense of survival, the like of which I had never needed before, lashing out in defence at the blurred figure any time he came near.

Where's the referee? Why hadn't he stepped in? Why was he allowing my opponent to continue? All questions that would not be answered whilst I worked hard to avoid his punches by using speed of foot and, to be honest, pure reactions. This rejuvenated opponent was now on the offensive.

'Protect yourselves at all times' is part of the pre-fight instructions. But this! This is the dark side of boxing that is generally only associated with professionals, not amateurs.

I almost shouted for joy as the bell sounded to bring this farce of a round to an end, and almost ran to my corner, plonking myself down on the stool that was waiting.

'Dirty little baarstad,' was Freddie's first comment as he swilled my face and then ran half a bottle of water across my open eye. He had obviously seen the incidents, so why hadn't the ref? 'You're not used to this, Ray.' More a statement than a question.

'Never experienced anything like it,' I retorted. 'What's the matter with the referee? Is he blind?'

'You'll not be getting any change from him, it's his brother's lad you're fighting tonight.' Freddie's remark came as a shock. Should that ever be allowed, I wondered?

No wonder the fight promoter had emphasised the word '*if*' I was to win, whilst telling me about the prize for the winner.

The cards seemed to be well and truly stacked in my opponent's favour, but then he had probably never fought a Yorkshireman before. 'From Rotherham, even,' I thought.

My eye was beginning to clear as the bell sounded to commence round two.

Now able to see fairly clearly, determined not to let my temper run wild and affect my fighting skills, I set about my opponent with more effort than I could ever remember.

The fire was now well and truly stoked, assisting with the power of my punches that were hurting him. I can't remember ever hitting the heavy punch bag with as much power. 'He doesn't like that,' I thought, as I landed with a cracking left hook just under his right ribs.

I could hear the grunts of expelled air as I pummelled his body and, from a very upright stance, he was now beginning to stoop. As the round progressed, his face, now on a level with mine, became a perfect target.

Just a token amount of retaliation coming from him kept me on my toes and, from a telegraphed right cross which I slipped over my left shoulder, I was able to connect another wicked left hook to his body. I followed this with the perfect right cross, a little high again, but this time he hit the canvas, trying desperately to grab hold of me on the way down.

I backed away and watched the countdown formality from a neutral corner. Slow to get started, but I was expecting him to be counted out. Whilst I waited, a flash of memory, like pressing rewind on a film, provided me with the answer to why my eye was so sore.

After my opponent had coated the soles of his boxing boots in the resin tray, he had then bent down, picked up the tray and handed it to his trainer. Something I would never have done, but obviously that's how he had managed to coat his gloves with the resin powder.

'Baarstad,' I muttered to myself, a much-used comment I had heard during the conversations in my London surroundings. It actually sounds more like a compliment than a swear word, the way it was delivered by the Cockneys.

I watched in disbelief as the referee performed the slowest of counts that seemed to have lasted at least thirty seconds! Even then, when my opponent rose at the extended count of nine, the ref made a longer job of cleaning his gloves than a professional cleaner would have taken to vacuum the bloody hall we were fighting in!

My opponent wasn't counted out.

What did I have to do to win this one?

Within less than half a minute of the fight being resumed, the bell sounded to end the round, with me chasing him around the ring trying to put this fight to bed.

Danny's words were echoing in my brain. 'You don't get paid overtime in this game. Get it over with and get out.'

Sam commented that I was well in front (on points) and just needed to stay in control. However, Freddie suggested, between sponging me down and giving me a soothing neck massage, that the only way I could guarantee a win was to "take him out". A new phrase. He was right, I needed to take him out, especially in view of the biased actions of his "uncle", the referee.

My eye was now clear and, although a little sore, was feeling as good as new after a couple of blinks and the last eye wash during the midway interval.

Freddie and Sam had done a great job; I couldn't have asked for a better away team. These two professionals were, without doubt, definitely in my corner and would have come to my rescue if required.

I was determined that, after listening to those comments to take him out, my opponent was about to feel the full impact of my skills. I stepped out of my corner and literally charged across the ring towards him, letting loose with a barrage of continuous punches that found their target like a homing device.

Covering up, he backed peddled into his own corner, where instructions of 'grab him, grab hold' were coming from his corner men. But I wasn't getting pulled into that clinching situation again. Every time he tried to grab hold, I stepped back one and then forward one with a punch and literally hammered an undefended face.

'Listen to your corner men,' I was thinking, because every time he tried to reach out to grab hold of me it left him unguarded and vulnerable.

I just knew that it wasn't going to last long. I wouldn't allow him to grab hold and could see the panic in his eyes, because I was scoring heavily with every telling punch.

I was right. I wouldn't allow him to get out of his corner and, no matter what he did and despite all the instructions from his panicking corner men, the fight was ended by a right uppercut that found its spot on his chin. He fell forward and, luckily, I managed to hold back a left hook that, although it was on the way, wasn't needed.

I knew he wasn't about to get up. The uppercut came from my toes, with just the right amount of twist from the hips and connected with the power that only correct timing achieves. Sometimes you just know!

I felt justified in feeling smug, as I watched this very biased referee count him out in super-quick time on this occasion, finishing the count just before the corner men had jumped into the ring to assist my cheating opponent.

My team were punching the air with clenched fists as I walked back towards them with the biggest satisfied grin on my face. 'Super job' and 'well done' greeted me from Sam and Freddie.

The MC jumped into the ring and, after a couple of minutes, whilst giving my opponent time to recover, started to make the announcement. Once again, the showbiz drawl of his lengthy statement was that, 'The winner by a knockout in the third round, all the way from Yorkshire' – near enough – 'Raaaaaaaaay Matthews.'

That time, the crowd did make a huge noise in my favour.

I walked over to my adversary's corner and reluctantly shook his and his coaches' hands, before footing the middle rope for him to exit the ring.

I was on top of the world, feeling satisfied and pleased that I had been able to rise above the unscrupulous antics of my opponent. I did, though, make a mental note that it wouldn't be such a bad idea to learn more about that dark side of the boxing game so that I could be ready for any future incidents.

After climbing out of the ring, Sam shadowed me as I walked over to the presentation table alongside the judging and timekeeping officials where the promoter and sponsor were seated.

I realised that Freddie had disappeared just before I collected the beautifully boxed ladies; Timex nine-carat gold watch which was officially presented to me by, as I later found out, the wife of the promoter who had made the '*if* you should win' comment earlier.

'This will look great on my mum's wrist,' I said to Sam as I showed him the contents of the box. The box alone looked a million dollars with its silky crimson lining and the Timex logo embossed in gold on the centre of the lid.

I was being stopped and congratulated at every other row of spectators, as I slowly made my way back to my changing room. Sam opened the door in front of me, almost bumping into Freddie, who was stood waiting for me.

'Ray, how would you fancy doing couple of exhibition rounds for us?' In total bewilderment, I didn't answer, so he continued. 'The promoter has just asked me to ask, as one of the bouts has been cancelled at late notice.'

I was gobsmacked. 'When?' I asked.

'Be around ten o'clock tonight.' That was just over an hour away.

'It will only be an exhibition bout with a young boy who needs a bit of boxing and ring experience. He's only had a couple of fights,' Freddie said.

I looked at him and smiled, well, I think I was probably smirking. I guess he knew what I was thinking. Once bitten, twice shy. I had nearly been bitten less than fifteen minutes ago.

Introduction to boxing's dark side

'No, it's genuine, Ray. Honest. He's about your weight and I train this young lad myself. You could do him the world of good. He's a bit cocky and it would be great to give him a bit of ring experience.

'Oh, and there's a tenner in it for you. He's outside if you want to meet him.'

It's funny how things happen and your mind picks up on certain things. I had only recently been talking to an ex-Londoner about the Cockney slang words used for different values of money.

'Not a pony, then?' I said, bursting out laughing, and a proper belly laugh at that. I nearly ended up on the floor at the thought of taking a pony back with me on the train to Doncaster and then on the bus back home to Rotherham.

Once again Freddie, who obviously didn't understand my Yorkshire humour, seriously thought that I had actually reckoned that a pony was indeed an animal, not an amount of money. How very different were our senses of humour?

'Bring him in,' I said to Freddie, giving this situation some thought while waiting.

It would only be like fighting in the championships, where you are likely to take on at least two opponents before the final. If this young lad was as inexperienced as Freddie had made out, then it would be a doddle.

Under normal circumstances, with Jacky by my side, I probably wouldn't have hesitated. But the real question was, did I trust Freddie? I decided that as long as this young boy wasn't a re-incarnation of Joe Louis or a Bruce Lee protégé, I should be able to cope.

The door opened again and in walked Freddie, together with the promoter and the so-called boy, who I suspected was no less than a month younger than me, probably already left or ready for leaving school.

'You'd be doing us a big favour, Ray,' said the smart-looking promoter guy. 'One of our fighters has had to go home poorly and we're down on bouts. There's a tenner in it for you,' he said. I subdued a laugh; he would never understand.

'OK, just as long as he knows that it's an exhibition and not a full-blown competition,' I replied, looking directly at my next sparring companion.

Freddie left to fetch Sam, who would be looking after my corner, the bout would be set for 10pm, just before the heavyweights.

The younger boy was, as Freddie had said, around my weight and height, but he looked a bit wild as he stared at me without flinching, when I had looked in his direction. Bravado, I suspected. I would probably have done the same myself if I had been in his shoes. Having now seen him, I had less of a reason to think this was a set-up. What's the worst that could happen?

I would just have to fight, that's all.

Sam arrived a few minutes later and, after his very complimentary comments about the previous fight, my ego was well and truly boosted. I liked this softly spoken guy who looked more like a proper bruiser, come minder, than some I had seen in films.

Again, with time to kill, we talked about fighting, and in particular about bare-knuckle fighting. The real problem was that facial cuts and old wounds would easily open up from knuckle-on-skin contact, often with very little force.

God, it sounded a brutal business that offered only small rewards at some of the street venues.

'Attract a big crowd and the rewards are worth the pain,' he said.

'Hell, Sam, was it all worth it?' I asked.

Of course, his answer was a resounding yes, and that he'd do it all again if given the chance.

Time had flown along whilst I had been enthralled listening to Sam and, as a reminder that fight time was close, the MC poked his head round the door and asked if we were ready.

'Two minutes,' Sam replied, as he turned to me with a look that said, is that OK? I nodded and headed for the toilet that I had been wanting to use for the past half hour but couldn't tear myself away from our conversation. I was enthralled and didn't want to miss a word.

I had kept the bandages on that were comfortably securing my hands, which meant that I was ready to go once Sam had laced up the gloves.

This time, the walk down the hall, with Sam leading, resulted in a huge cheer from the crowd, especially after they had been informed of my decision to stay and take on this exhibition bout.

My new challenger was already in the ring waiting for me, as I climbed up into the same corner as I had fought from an hour and a half ago. Sam followed me and stood on the outside apron waiting for the proceedings to start.

Once again, the MC performed his showbiz-style announcement after talking about me generously agreeing to take part in this forthcoming exhibition bout and helping to fill the bill, which resulted in another rousing cheer from the now-friendly crowd.

The biased referee was back, signalling us to approach

the centre of the now-familiar ring to be advised on the dos and don'ts of this one-off bout. During this time my younger opponent tried to outstare me. 'The young whipper-snapper.' I smiled. After shaking gloved hands, we retired to our corners.

Sam had managed to scrounge a clean towel from someone and, after a quick face swill, patted my damp skin and swung the towel round his neck.

After placing the moist gum shield in my mouth, Sam exited the ring with a thumbs-up sign. Two or three seconds later, the bell rang to get this non-competitive exhibition bout underway.

I had to suppress a laugh as this so-called novice came rushing towards me, straight from the bell, with swinging arms trying to knock me out.

'Whoa,' I shouted in his face as I tied him up in my corner, trapping his arms close to his body. '

'Steady yourself down,' I shouted in his ear before backing off and letting him go. But he obviously hadn't heeded my warning as he was coming at me again.

The crowd was in hysterics. They all appeared to be taking part in this farcical opening few seconds, at the instant attack from my younger opponent who clearly wanted to make an impression.

I backed off and let him swing his energy away into mid-air. Swing after swing, miss after miss I could see his temper rising even that early into the round. He was also, like most, lacking in fight fitness as he slowly ran out of steam.

It was time to really show him what this boxing malarkey is all about.

He had come to a complete standstill well before the end

of the round, as I hit him with more punches than I expected he had ever witnessed before.

None of the punches were meant to hurt, nor was it my intention to connect with any force. This meant that I could concentrate on the sort of speed that he couldn't even keep pace with. He needed to be taught a lesson, I was thinking, as I flicked out punches rather than punched.

The first round ended with my younger opponent gasping for breath and staggering back to his corner. But instead of going back to mine, I followed him across to his waiting coach.

Freddie had jumped into the ring to take care of his boy and guide him back to his stool. I gave him the evil eye and told him to have a word with his boy. 'Sorry,' mouthed Freddie, as I turned and walked back to Sam, who was grinning from ear to ear.

As I stood facing him, Sam took and swilled my gum shield and, without saying a word, offered me a bottle of water to swill my mouth. I had even managed to raise a sweat after that last minute of speed work.

Gum shield sucked in and a final swing of the towel to agitate the cooler air, Sam patted me on the back, left the outside apron and took up position on the hall floor to watch. He hadn't uttered a single word.

Round two started out in a much calmer manner. I was happy to allow my younger, inexperienced opponent to keep throwing punches at me but never allowed him to actually connect. I blocked and moved out of reach, in order to show him that he would need to use his feet as well as his fists.

This bout was now more comfortable and on par with my training sessions with our young novices at home. More in line with what I had expected when I had agreed to take part in the exhibition bout.

Towards the middle of the round, as with round one, the now ill-tempered young boxer was blowing out of his backside and, once again, as the round progressed, started to lose his temper big-style.

'No, you don't,' I said as he tried to swing a full-blown right-hander that was intended to take my head of my shoulders. 'Wrong attitude!' I shouted in his ear as I had him pinned in his corner, with Freddie also shouting for him to calm down. He was never going to learn anything using this uncooperative behaviour. Well, certainly not from me. I was not in the ring to be used as a punch bag for anyone.

The round came to an end with my gasping young opponent lying on the ropes in despair, trying to recover from half a minute of him desperately attempting to stop me from finding gaps in his defence. He had even brought his left knee up on a couple of occasion to lessen the gap to his body.

Once again, I walked over to Freddie and asked him if his boy had had enough. They had mentioned a couple of rounds, and unless our Yorkshire 'couple of rounds' was anything different than those in London, then this exhibition fight should now have come to a conclusion.

'Fancy another round?' Freddie asked his young protégé, who, to my surprise, said yes. Gutsy, to say the least. I wasn't expecting that.

Before I turned back to Sam for the last round, I gave Freddie one of those looks that said many things, which he acknowledged with a wink and a nod.

Whatever Freddie had said to his young fighter had

worked. I was more than happy to let him come at me with more controlled punches.

I felt sure that if he was to train harder and work on his temper, over time he could become a half-decent fighter. If nothing else, he certainly wasn't lacking in guts.

I was more inclined to let him punch at my stomach without blocking his very tired attempts. He was finding it difficult to move, never mind keep up with his sparring, as his punches came to a complete standstill.

As I tied my young opponent up on the ropes above the official table, I was able to catch the eye of the timekeeper, signalling for him bring the round to an end well before it was time.

My unfit opponent was spent, gasping for breath and had run out of steam, seriously showing signs of collapsing through sheer exertion. I was almost forced to keep him propped up on the ropes above the timekeeper until the bell rang.

Freddie, who had jumped into the ring, met me yards away from his corner and took over supporting his young fighter.

I followed Freddie out of concern as his young protégé, who was still fighting for breath, plonked himself heavily on the stool. I stayed for a while and asked if he was OK. He just about managed a nod as I made my way back to my corner to a smiling Sam.

The night came to an end with me refusing to accept the tenner but delighted with the new watch and the promise that the cash would be donated to a local charity for old soldiers.

My first-ever charity fundraising event, I believe!

Sam and I hugged, shook hands for the last time and

promised to keep in touch. Sadly, I lost his address when the cellar at home in Masbrough flooded after a water pipe burst. This was some months after my London trip and destroyed many old boxing photos, letters and boxing prizes.

When I look back on my London adventure and put pen to paper, so to speak, I believe this experience, more than any other, helped me mature. It would no doubt become invaluable when the time came for me to turn pro.

10

Two marathons, one civic reception

Une bonne idée is what the French call a good idea. I thought I'd had one of those ten months before starting the marathons. But that day had finally arrived and it was sending shivers down my spine.

It was time for our trip to France, a trip which would hopefully add to the overall fundraising draw and credibility of my challenge. You will recall, this double-marathon weekend had been organised some months earlier during a flying visit to our friends at the ACPI running club.

I was now questioning my sanity and wondering if I had made the right decision to run the fiftieth and fifty-first marathons on French soil. But I didn't have much time to ponder as they were now looming closer. In fact, just over twenty-four hours away.

The journey, an almost eight hundred-mile round trip to Saint-Quentin in France, was weighing heavily on my mind.

Ready or not, shortly before 6am, after a fitful night's sleep, I set off to run and complete the forty-ninth consecutive marathon. It was a Friday, meaning it would be the last one in the UK until Monday morning! I was aiming to complete this marathon in under five hours, which should easily be achievable without any interruptions.

At that time in the morning, the weather was much cooler than I had become used to over the past month and a half as I set off into a slight drizzle. I jogged down my drive and headed right, then left down through the lichen gate of St Bartholomew's Church.

Ducking under the low brow of the old yew tree and on to the well-worn path, I headed out towards the Maltby Crags. Uttermost on my mind was getting back home – safely, on time and injury-free – before midday with at least 26.2 miles registered on my Garmin watch.

Although I was feeling as fit as a butcher's dog at this juncture, certainly more than capable of a sub-four-hour marathon, I needed to concentrate on the discipline of a steady pace.

I settled on running at just over a ten-minute mile pace, as running faster could have resulted in muscle tension – or worse!

With such an important weekend beckoning, it was imperative to conclude this early start lone marathon injury-free.

Running a cross-country marathon around Maltby was never going to be easy as, by definition, the very phrase cross-country means there are no flat areas. I had decided a few days earlier that my best option would be to head out towards Roche Abbey and down the valley line into Stone, on to Firbeck and out towards Langold, some five miles away.

The idea was then to run around the circumference of this picturesque lake which has an exact one-mile path. Langold was ideal because it provided reasonably flat running where I could clock up the miles at a steady constant pace before it was time to head back home.

If all went well, I was expecting to be back home within four and a half hours, which would give me ample time to get ready for the long journey across the Channel.

The morning's marathon run had gone according to plan. Just under four hours and twenty-five minutes after leaving the house I was enjoying a bite to eat after a quick, refreshing shower.

It would soon be time to meet the coach-load of friends, running colleagues and supporters who would be accompanying me over the next two and a bit days during our journey into France.

Just before midday, dragging our weekend case that Maureen had prepared and kit bag full of running gear, we locked our back door. Walking the few hundred yards in the drizzling rain up the lane onto Blyth Road, we were welcomed on board the twenty-nine-seater coach, already full of our friends.

Before we set off, team photos were the order of the day, as Dave Poucher organised some of our party into an orderly group alongside the bus, with the French flag fluttering in the breeze. The photo would appear in following week's local and very supportive Rotherham Advertiser.

As we made our way up the relatively new coach, through enthusiastic comments and handshakes from our friends, I could see that the full back seat had been left for Maureen and me. This would allow plenty of room to spread out during our long journey across the channel to Saint-Quentin.

We settled down shortly after getting underway, with Maureen taking up the nearside section of the back seat, leaving me the remainder to chill out and get as much rest as possible. This was not something I was good at or had much practice of late, but I closed my eyes, hoping to get some rest.

As the bus quietened down and with the hypnotic steady drone of the road noise, I must have drifted off because, all of a sudden, I awoke sweating cobs and recalling what I had dreamt about. A nightmare centring on the forthcoming event not going too well.

I was having shivers about the French trip and had woken with a feeling of trepidation and despair that during this weekend of daily marathons, over which I had minimal control, many things could go wrong and jeopardise the overall challenge that was so close to reaching a successful conclusion.

'What if?'

What if I was to pick up an injury that I couldn't deal with? What would happen if the coach broke down and we were stranded on the other side of the Channel and I couldn't complete the marathons? What would happen if we couldn't get home? There must have been a dozen or so things that could have gone wrong and brought this challenge crashing down.

I think my subconscious must have been filtering the many comments that had been innocently made over the past few days, but in my short dream, having analysed rightly or wrongly, I must have added two and two and made five.

People in their dozens had wished me good luck, with

comments of 'stay safe', 'take care' and 'hope all goes well while you're in France'. All statements which had a hint that things could possibly go wrong. I had woken up in a panic: a controlled panic if that makes sense. There was a full weekend ahead which, rather than being in my control, would be in other people's hands. I would be totally reliant on good fortune and enthusiastic company to bring this additional challenge to a successful conclusion.

Whoa. This wasn't like me. I am that Yorkshireman, after all, who ran 150 miles in one go within thirty-six hours, just less than four years ago. I had successfully dealt with many 'on-the-go' problems to bring an even greater challenge to a triumphant conclusion.

Never negative, I have always been that positive glass-half-full guy who's always in control of his thoughts and actions.

I was determined that this was going to be a great, successful weekend, one which would create amazing memories that I would be able to treasure for the rest of my life. I needed to dismiss those crazy, negative thoughts out of my head.

'Whatever happens, I will deal with it. Sorted!'

All this seriousness and we had only just passed the outskirts of Worksop on the A1, less than twenty miles into the trip!

I settled back down and began reminiscing over the past eighteen months or so, of how my life had dramatically changed.

I had become a salesman of sorts, selling much more than a product by asking people to buy into a dream, my dream. A dream that had completely taken over my normal life, turning into something that I could never have imagined possible. Then there was the pressure that hung over it, the like of which I had never experienced before.

A complete novice to this new way of life, I was prepared and willing to go along on this merry-go-round, although it was like living in a goldfish bowl. Everyone could see my every waking day's movements, although I realised some time ago, this would become necessary if we were to achieve the enormous target of seventy-five thousand pounds.

With lots of travelling time in front of me, my thoughts turned to the amazing response I had received from sponsors, before and during the earlier marathons. The sponsors had played a major part of our success to date. People who had shown faith, believing that I would undoubtedly deliver on my promise and, equally as important, were prepared to back it up by putting money on it.

Friends and running clubs had become a big part of the challenge, not only by sponsoring me but spending time organising full-distance marathons, as well as recruiting club runners to accompany me during the events.

A big shout out to Kimberworth Striders, Clowne RC, Team Manvers, Rotherham Harriers, Valley Hill Runners, Worksop Harriers and, my own club at that time, Maltby RC. A profound thanks not only for the money donated but also for providing the great memories of running with friends.

Contributions, too, from individuals and the many local businesses that had freely helped to fill up the marathon sponsor calendar. Our dedicated website had been filling up fast from these generous people. I will be eternally grateful to the many local businesses who took up our plight and donated via our marathon calendar boxes; all deserve a mention and can be accessed on www.rwrr.co.uk.

Two marathons, one civic reception

I was conscious that the coach had come to complete standstill, well before reaching Cambridge and the M11 motorway, with the usual Friday-afternoon nose-to-tail traffic. Eventually, after a few minutes' worrying about missing the ferry, we began inching forward and finally joined the dreaded M25 motorway which, luckily, was in full flow, much to my surprise.

We crossed over the Dartford Queen Elizabeth II Bridge, standing at around 140 metres above the Thames. This magnificent structure was completed around 1990, massively easing the estuarial traffic.

This bridge is a great feat of engineering, when you consider the vast curve from both sides that came together when the last middle section was erected. The main span across the Thames is just under half a mile long.

I was able to witness this bridge being constructed every day, watching it grow for around five months whilst I was working near there constructing a number of industrial units on the south-eastern side of Dartford, alongside the old oil storage depot.

Construction to the warehouses was halted for an hour during the afternoon whilst we watched the last section of the bridge being erected in place from below.

The M20 on our way into Dover seemed to take forever, but we finally headed into the entrance of the P&O Ferry terminal and, having just missed our allocated ferry, we settled down to wait for the next available one.

Conscious of the impending late arrival into Saint-Quentin, at least our coach was positioned at the front of the queue and eventually we led the way up the gantry onto the boat.

We landed in France a couple of hours later after a fairly smooth crossing and quickly left the ferry terminal in Calais behind and headed out on the E15. This quiet road links into the tolled motorway network and eventually takes you via an almost double loop to the outskirts of Saint-Quentin.

We arrived at our hotel, Le Florence on Rue Emile Zola, close to 2am.

The hotel staff were waiting to greet us as a phone call had been made advising them of our impending delay.

The majority of our party booked into Le Florence, while the remainder of the group headed further up the road to their hotel close to the town centre.

Our room at Le Florence, part of the newly renovated old coach house building, which Maureen and I had used on a number of occasions over the years, provided the familiarity that makes it more homely. It's reassuring knowing where everything is which meant that we could dive into bed after setting the alarm for 7am, now less than five hours away.

Hopefully we could get some sleep before it was time for Dominique to pick me up, but can you ever get to sleep when you're trying hard? Afraid not. It didn't happen, and before I knew it, that awful shrill from the alarm sounded. Time to get up, head to the dining room for breakfast and then get ready to run a marathon!

After breakfast, Dominique was waiting in reception and, after our greeting, drove me down from our hotel through familiar streets and across the imposing Riqueval Bridge. This area saw one of the greatest British battles of World War I on 29th September 1918 to capture the bridge.

A large crowd was already gathering as we parked up in a reserved space in the car park.

I was welcomed by long-standing French friends, Jean-Claude, Christian and Freddy, along with Jean-Marc, who managed to run one of the full marathons with me, and Jose, on his bike, with his funny 'ay-up' interpretation of a Yorkshire dialect greeting that Maureen had coached him on a couple of years before.

I reckon a good thirty runners and a few on their bikes were waiting at the park, mostly old friends who had been following the progress of my marathons and who would be running part of or all of the two marathons with me.

Some of our British group were arriving at the park to run with us as I was being introduced to Jacky Lesueur and his wife, both distance runners. This amazing couple had heard about my challenge and had travelled more than 150km to run the two marathons with me. What a humbling experience. We have become good friends over the years since.

Maureen would be coming down to support me later with a number of our travelling friends to keep her company, after first soaking up the experience of Saint-Quentin around the pre-set route that was very familiar to her.

The sun was shining bright as we lined up and then, after a very informal countdown, headed out of the park shortly after 9am on the first of the two marathons.

We set off running out of the park towards the Riqueval Bridge, passing the newly refurbished war memorial wall, before turning sharp some quarter of a mile away onto the well-maintained wide canal towpath.

The canal which runs through Saint-Quentin, named the Canal de Picardie, links the River Escaut at Cambrai to the Canal de l'Oise at Chauny and flows for a distance of just over 92km. I believe it was opened by Napoleon himself in 1810.

The Path to Success

What an amazing and humbling sight as I turned my head and looked back after about half a mile or so to see the line of brightly coloured runners and bikers following me like the Pied Piper! We even had our very own official ACPI photographer who kept popping up around the route, taking action shots as we passed.

The first of the photos came from a bridge over the canal which the French runners were all aware of, as they seemed to pose on cue to capture a cracking photo!

Leaving the canal behind after the best part of three miles, we made a sharp right turn up the bank side and shortly after, in glorious sunshine, ran through Omissy and Morcourt, two very typical French villages. We then made our way through a wooded area back to the park, where Maureen, Jim Southern, Michele and Geoff Vincent were waiting to cheer us on.

The newly established zoo enclosure, either side of the main path, looked to have matured from the previous year and now contained a larger variety of animals, I was informed, as we ended our first loop at the checkpoint and drink station to an enthusiastic French and British crowd.

I was keen to get underway again shortly after a drink of water. For this next lap I would be joined by some new ACPI runners who more than made up for the few who had retired after the first of the four clockwise laps, and were keen and ready to continue on this very pleasant ten and a bit-kilometre loop.

Jean-Claude informed me during the second loop that I was to be invited to a civic reception in my honour later this afternoon around 4pm, at the Saint-Quentin town hall, situated in the very impressive town centre square.

I had already had first-hand experiences of these formal

receptions over the years as part of the Maltby Running Club team and recalled how time-consuming they could be! Nevertheless, what an honour for me to be the recipient of this impending civic reception. It was going to be a long day!

The fiftieth marathon came to an end sometime before 3pm, just by the church of Rouvroy, one of the small churches in the village. Shortly after, I was whisked away back to our hotel, where Maureen was waiting after a busy day for her.

A quick shower and change and we were ready for our short walk into the town centre, across the large town square and into the main entrance of the large town hall where we all congregated.

Our group was met inside the main entrance by the welcoming committee. After photos of us all behind a large ACPI banner just outside the main entrance, we were escorted up the wide ornate staircase into a large, imposing reception room. This elegant room housed some of the famous Rococo Portrait paintings by Maurice Quentin from around the 1700s. Dominating this high-ceilinged room stood a massive ornate light grey marble fireplace.

Champagne, nuts and nibbles were on offer as we stood around talking and waiting for the proceedings to begin.

It was great to meet up with many of my ACPI running-club friends, all of whom had been invited to share the evening with me. Together with all the British visitors, we filled the room to the rafters.

Alexis Grandin, president of the Office of Tourism at the congress of Saint-Quentin, arrived. He kick-started the civic reception by joining the line-up of ACPI committee members and, of course, me! I was coaxed to the front, lining up for official photos with the press and TV cameras.

I was made a 'proper fuss of', as we say in Yorkshire, for over an hour and a half with comments that needed interpretation in order for us all to understand.

Alexis and then Jean-Claude made their speeches of welcome and amazement of the overall challenge, of which they were proud to have been part. This left me to make an improvised, impromptu response, made all the more difficult because of the translation delays.

The evening was destined to be a long affair, as every word needed translation either one way or the other, admirably performed by Dominique's son, Quentin. He had spent some time as part of a Rotherham student exchange scheme, I believe, and lived as a guest in Rotherham a few years before.

By the time words were exhausted, interviews had been carried out and we'd mingled for some time, I suddenly realised that it was nearing ten o'clock. Neither Maureen nor I had eaten a proper meal since that morning's breakfast! Not conducive for running marathons.

A group of us managed to persuade, in our best pleading voices, a town centre restaurant to remain open and feed us. After pizza, chips and a pint of local lager, we headed back to our hotel just before midnight. Time to catch up with a few hours of sleep before Dominique would be collecting me at 8:30 in the morning for the fifty-first marathon.

During our meal, and for the first time in hours, we were able to catch up. Maureen was in stitches telling me later that they had twice ended up in a betting shop, thinking it was a cafe! Coffee was being served inside as they watched people putting on bets and the group were invited to join them for coffee. It would have been rude not to!

All too soon, that dreaded alarm was ringing in my ears after only a few hours of – I was about to say sleep, but in reality it was just rest. I couldn't come down from the high and thoughts about the concluding marathon on French soil.

'Who's about to run another marathon then?'

On arrival at the park, I was met with a rousing cheer and warm greeting from the French runners and some of the Brits who were about to complete a lap or two with me. Of the British contingent, Caroline Boyd had managed the full marathon the previous day.

Everyone wanted photos of this unique occasion, which took up quite some time, during which I was presented with a large shoe box which was completely covered with the brightly coloured flyers that had been used to promote the fundraising in Saint-Quentin. The box contained loads of Euros that the club had collected for me.

Dominique agreed to bank transfer the cash over to our Golden Giving site and save me the hassle of exchanging the Euros and then banking the converted cash. After all, he was a highly positioned bank manager so it was the least he could do!

What an amazing second marathon: run in blazing sun, which we all managed to complete by following the same route as the day before, thought to be best and safest.

I was accompanied once again by a large group, including a young ACPI lady who managed to run her first full marathon with me. She was ecstatic by the time we reached the Rouvroy Church on the last lap.

We were greeted by a large crowd of French spectators, a yard or two beyond the church, at the house of one the runners. Tables of food, wine and ice-cold lager were on offer at the roadside.

It was tempting to just stay and gorge myself and soak up all the accolades that were being given out. However, time was marching on and I needed to return to the coach, where my friends would be waiting to make the long trip home. That ice-cold lager was just magic.

Dominique drove me back to where the coach was parked and, after an emotional farewell, we bade our French friends au revoir and made our way out of Saint-Quentin, heading for the motorway and the port of Calais.

The French customs were a complete nightmare to get through, as we finally reached the border gate.

We were all made to leave the coach and walk through the customs shed whilst the coach was searched. That was followed by an even longer delay at the hands of the UK Border Control while still on French soil. This seemed nothing more than a farcical one-upmanship effort to catch out the French as they (re)searched bags, checked and double-checked our documents.

Making matters worse, we were then held up in the document check shed because of a large group of foreign children wanting to enter the UK. Both the large group in front and our party were being processed by a single official, who was being over-cautious with everyone's documents.

Of course, we missed our scheduled sailing and had to wait for the next available ferry.

Eventually, our coach boarded the ferry and, just over two and a half hours later, we docked after another smooth crossing and made our way out of the P&O Dover ferry port onto the M20 and hotfooted it home.

After a short compulsory stop at a service station, we arrived back in Maltby around 1am Monday morning, which meant that most of the rest of our party wouldn't see their beds before 2am.

What an amazing, eventful and memorable weekend the French marathons turned out to be.

Time for bed for Maureen and me. There was another marathon waiting for me the next day. Well, actually, in a few hours that same day!

*

Guest Contribution

Dominique Dubreuil, ACPI Running Club

Sport, and in particular running, automatically creates a sense of camaraderie and friendship that even crosses language barriers no matter where you are in the world. This was the case when we first visited Saint-Quentin, our French-twinned town, where Maureen and I first met Dominique and the local ACPI running club members. Over the past fifteen years or so we have formed a great friendship with Dominique that has grown year on year.

Ray Matthews

At the end of March 2008, as part of the twinning between Saint-Quentin and Rotherham, ACPI (Association des Coureurs du Parc d'Isle) hosted, for the first time, English runners from Maltby Running Club.

About twenty English runners made the trip, which was our first experience of welcoming a foreign delegation, and we stayed at the youth hostel, men on one side, women on the other.

Sunday morning was our race day. There were 237 runners who started our 15km race, where the fastest finished the course within fifty minutes.

At the end of the peloton of runners was a short man, the veteran of our race, running at his own pace, sporting the 19 bib on his vest. He did not seem to be suffering and gave the impression of taking his time, having fun and enjoying the landscape. That day Ray finished last.

At that moment, no one imagined that he would return eight years later for a huge challenge and a great life lesson of courage and self-denial.

Exchanges between French and English runners throughout the years developed a strong friendship. It is always a joy for ACPI to welcome MRC runners to Saint-Quentin and a great pleasure to go to England and run together.

In these exchanges, we have seen in Ray immense fighting spirit, learned from his past as a boxer and his work as an engineer.

At the beginning of 2016, Ray informed us that he was going to take on an incredible challenge and run seventy-five marathons in seventy-five days, starting on his seventy-fifth birthday. His target? To raise money for the Newman School. Naturally, he thought of his French friends and offered to run two marathons in Saint-Quentin during August.

Two days in France were necessary to make a journey of over 600km possible and allow Ray to recover a little on his return journey, before the continuation of his challenge in England.

Being a thorough man, Ray made a visit in February 2016 in Saint-Quentin. Jean-Claude, the President of ACPI, arranged

Two marathons, one civic reception

for him to meet the local press. Ray explained his motives and why he decided to do us the honour of running in Saint-Quentin. It is all in the head, he says, he is the man who dares.

We drove him around the surrounding countryside to determine the route.

Months passed, Ray was training, and then his seventy-fifth birthday was approaching. The challenge started. We kept in touch with him and closely followed his progress in the challenge.

We hoped that the two marathons in Saint-Quentin would meet his expectations, both sporting and human. We organised a fundraiser to contribute financially to the challenge.

Ray arrived by coach, but he was not alone, accompanied by runners from several clubs to support him in France.

Meanwhile, work on a bridge required us to modify the circuit with the finish now at the church of Rouvroy, after four laps of our usual route along the canal and the villages of Omissy and Morcourt.

We planned refreshments with French runners join Ray and the English runners. Jean-Marc ran the total of one of the marathons with Ray. A couple of runners even travelled over 100km to run with Ray. Others ran one or two laps.

In the middle of the afternoon of the first day, Ray accepted an invitation to the town hall in his honour. We would have liked to have celebrated the fiftieth marathon with him, but we knew he had to rest.

After too short a night, Ray arrived at the entrance of the Parc d'Isle, and started running, running, running…

At the end of the fifty-first marathon, he had to return, by coach, to England, where the challenge continued. We would have liked to have spent some time with him, but we knew that it was not possible. We promised to follow him on social networks and would always have the pleasure of seeing him in our next exchanges.

À *bientôt*, Ray.

*

Guest Contribution

Michele Vincent

Thank you for being a valued friend, Michele. From our very first meeting in the Costa in Parkgate shopping centre, where I had no hesitation to ask you to help with the editing of Who Dares, as well as the many times you have been there supporting at award ceremonies and events.

Ray Matthews

When I worked for the *Rotherham Advertiser* newspaper from 2000 until my retirement in 2014, I became aware of Ray Matthews. Ray, then retired, was not only a keen runner but also an author and a skilled artist, as well as being a Good Samaritan.

I think that the first story about Ray which I covered for the paper was when he accompanied a blind ex-serviceman on a run, acting as his guide. I also became aware of a book, *Me and My Shadow*, which he had written. When I read the book, I loved reading about the challenges which he faced, especially running in the Sahara Desert. I developed a great admiration for him.

Soon after I retired in April 2014, I was contacted by one of my former colleagues saying that Ray was looking for someone to proofread his second book.

We met and Ray asked me to proofread *Who Dares*. The book covered his ultra runs as well as anecdotes of his childhood and his early love of boxing. Ray found a publisher for *Who Dares* and later I was proud to accompany him to a book signing at St Ann's Leisure Centre. I, of course, have a copy of the book at home.

Never one to just sit down and take it easy, Ray decided on a challenge which sounded extraordinary – that of running seventy-five marathons in seventy-five consecutive days, starting at the time of his seventy-fifth birthday in 2016. I followed his progress on Facebook and saw that he was planning to run two marathons in Rotherham's twin town in France, Saint-Quentin. Ray had close links with the ACPI running club in the town.

My husband, Geoff, and I were delighted to be part of the group accompanying Ray and his wife, Maureen, to Saint-Quentin in August 2016. Ray has covered much of the story of the French marathons and our time in Saint-Quentin in the foregoing chapter, although I have to confess to being part of the group that explored the town with Maureen!

Maureen, Geoff and I had cheered him on his way and then I'm ashamed to say that not long afterwards, we retired to one of the local cafes for a coffee and quite possibly a cake, too!

At the end of the second marathon on French soil, we commenced our long return journey arriving, from memory, around 2am.

I'm very glad that I was given the opportunity to get to know Ray and I am proud to call him and Maureen friends.

11

Sammy returns to haunt me

Having had just over a month of competitive fight starvation and champing at the bit, I was excited to learn that our club, and in particular yours truly, had been invited to take part in a tournament that was to be held in Newcastle. This fight would take place in just over a month's time. Among the nine fighters requested, there was an opponent matched up for me.

Yay! A fight at last! It had been the longest inactive period of competitive fighting for me since starting out as an almost ten-year-old.

Whilst I sadistically enjoyed the rigorously tough training, I really loved fighting.

As a priority during my pre-fight training, to learn more about the shady, dirty side of boxing that I had experienced for the first time in London, I had travelled all the way to Blackpool to an ex-Navy officer friend of Jacky's called Chris Thompson. Chris, who coached and trained professionals from his boxing gym, had, as a favour to Jacky, agreed to put me through a crash course of the unsavoury side of the fighting game.

I was met at the Bloomfield Road bus station, close to the football stadium, and bussed to the gym somewhere north of the imposing Blackpool Tower. I spent the entire day and late into the evening with Chris, being taught how to use and, more importantly, avoid the dodgy practices of boxing. It was a crash course in every sense of the word, one which left me with a couple of bruises and lump on my left cheek.

'You have to become a sort of magician; speed and sleight of hand is how it works. Not to mention elbows and thumbs,' Chris said as our long day finally came to an end.

Reaction speed of the foul and understanding how to take evasive action was now part of my armoury. I felt ready for anything that could be thrown at me.

As time passed, I was slowly becoming one of the elder statesmen of the Phoenix Boxing Club squad – longevity, rather than age, mind. Time had slowly whittled down our impressive senior boxing team. There were now many more fighters with less experience than me.

The seniors, just three of them now but still a force to be reckoned with, were all ABA champions. Also, luckily for us there was always an up-and-coming newbie fighter somewhere in the country who was looking to take scalps, pretty much like I was early in my career. Fortunately, that's how we managed to pick up the odd fight.

Even though my next opponent must have been around for some time, I hadn't come across or heard of him. Reading the attached portfolio of my opponent, Jacky said that he had a pretty impressive record, recently winning an ABA title at nine and a half stone. That is just under lightweight but half a stone heavier than we were matched at.

I expressed my doubts to Jacky that he probably wouldn't manage to get down to the lower weight that we were due to fight at. You may remember that I had found it extremely difficult to lose just four ounces before the Yorkshire Schoolboy championships, let alone six pounds.

Maybe a misprint, or should I be concerned?

Billed as a Saturday evening boxing tournament, it meant that we would be staying up north overnight in Newcastle. Some of the young lads who were chosen to fight would experience the luxury of a four- or five-star hotel for the first time. Remember, only the best for the Phoenix Boxing Club.

I wouldn't have to be concerned about my brother Alan on this trip, as he would be away with some of his schoolmates on a pre-arranged working holiday. They were helping out on a farm somewhere near Youlgreave, in the Peak District, so I would only have myself to consider during this tournament.

We were picked up from the gym on Sheffield Road and boarded one of the latest, most luxurious coaches on the road at that time. Joining us were around twelve parents, which unusually included three mums. There were ten or so of our usual supporters, plus Jacky, Jimmy and Jack Cox.

Our team of mostly young fighters were all excited and showing nerves as we settled down on the packed coach. They were just kids, after all, their parents also rookies to fight tournaments. First-timers to this, an away-from-home competition. This was a big deal for most of the boys and parents.

Travelling up the busy A1 to Newcastle, we finally arrived at our destination late afternoon after a short tea break.

The hotel, nothing much to look at from the outside, opened up into an impressive cavernous interior of luxurious light grey marble and deep-pile red carpets.

We lined up facing the imposing, highly polished mahogany reception desk, almost as tall as me, to register and pick up our room keys. After providing my name, address details and signing in, I was handed a large key with my room number etched onto an oblong white fob. I was excited as I realised that, for the very first time, I had been allocated a room to myself.

My so-called single room was not only massive but turned out to be luxurious, the like of which I had never experienced before as I stepped inside the high-ceilinged, spacious room. After the long journey, first port of call was the bathroom, which turned out to be larger than our living room at home!

Try as I may, I can't remember the room number, but I'm sure it was on the fourth floor.

I settled in, laying out my boxing kit, towel and gum shield in a sort of ritual on the massive single bed. It's always best to double-check as, at that stage, I would have time to rectify anything I had forgotten to pack.

We all met shortly afterwards for tea and sandwiches in the dining room with mums and dads, noisily and excitedly exchanging pleasantries as I arrived downstairs.

I was pumped for information from a group of parents, enquiring about what to expect during the evening. As the new, unofficially appointed spokesman for the club, I tried my best to answer their questions in between mouthfuls of ham and cheese sandwiches.

After the light buffet, we were instructed to get ready so we could leave for the event centre on time.

Half an hour later, one by one our immaculately dressed team assembled in the lobby then boarded the coach: a very special occasion for some of the younger boys. After a head count, we set off for the venue, which was less than ten minutes away.

The impression we created as a team, once again, was awesome. All dressed in mid-grey slacks, white shirts with a dark blue tie under a navy-blue blazer displaying the bright red and gold Phoenix club badge on the breast pocket, we were a sight to behold.

We created a sight that made a bold statement: the Phoenix Boxing Club had arrived. And a sight that I was always proud to be part of.

Doors opened and people made way for us as we entered the imposing St James Boxing Hall. We were escorted to our team changing room at the far end of the hall by one of the event team.

I quickly claimed a corner spot and the rest of the team spread out like we owned the place. It was like an unspoken statement saying this room belonged to the Phoenix Boxing Club for the next four or five hours.

As I sat down to chill out, I could see the effect this old, sparsely decorated, purpose-built brick building, with fading pro fight and wrestling posters plastered around the walls, was having on some of our younger boys. It just reeked of fighting history; you could almost feel the ghosts of past performers.

Nerves were kicking in and adrenaline would be surging through their tense bodies. But that's normal and anyone who says they don't feel that rush of nerves must be dead. Even I got the heebie-jeebies during the early part of getting ready to fight, but it's all about using that adrenaline and turning it into positive power. Luckily, I have always been able to control my emotions. Ten minutes later, right on cue, I was calm and collected on the outside but like a coiled spring inside, ready to pull the trigger.

The question I have often wondered since is, would I have been that relaxed and chilled had I had known that that evening's fight in Newcastle was to be my very last? The very last time I would ever step into a ring to compete.

Stevie Boy, my opponent, was already at the front of the queue as we stood in line behind the old-fashioned weight scales in an anteroom that linked our changing rooms together.

Jacky, who was in close attendance standing near to the scales, managed to catch the weight announcement.

He shouted over, raising his arm, signalling me to join him at the front of line. 'Ray, can you weigh in now before we make the decision?' he asked as I joined him at the front of the queue by the side of the scales.

'Problem?' I asked, walking over alongside my opponent and his trainer who had coloured up.

'Looks like your opponent is about six pounds overweight,' Jacky exclaimed loud enough for everyone to hear!

We all came together in a circle around the front of the line-up, looking on as I stepped onto the archaic scales that took ages to settle.

Standing perfectly still, I breathed in as the guy in charge moved the pointer down the bar into position. I tipped the scales at a touch over nine stone. Spot on.

Our fight had been arranged at nine stone. I could have easily made the dead weight if needed as I was still fully dressed, except for shoes and jacket.

Jacky, his arm now around my shoulders, steered me to one side as I stepped off and away from the scales. 'Ray, you'll be giving away the best part of half a stone if we go ahead with this one tonight! But it's your choice.'

It seemed a bit of a fix to me and I wasn't surprised at all that my opponent was over the weight. But I was already in the fight zone, fired up and wasn't going to miss out on a fight having travelled all that way for nothing. I made the decision to go for it.

'OK, let's do it,' I said to Jacky.

We looked about the same height and similar build. But remembering that he had won the ABA championship at the nine-and-a-half-stone category two months previous, it came as no surprise that he would be heavier than me.

Sailing through the medical inspection, it was then time to chill out in the now fairly quiet changing room.

It seemed that the more relaxed I appeared, the more our younger fighters seemed to settle down. We enjoyed light-hearted conversations until it was time for each one of them in turn to get ready to fight.

My own fight was allocated a late spot on the bill and I reckoned that, if all the fights before me went to time, mine would be around ten o'clock. This meant I would be next to last to fight for our club.

Lots of time to ponder about the snap decision I had made, but also lots of time for my opponent to worry about me.

Heavyweights would then follow my fight, bringing the tournament to a close at around 10:40pm.

I was able to watch some of our young boys perform. Each one in turn did themselves and their club proud, winning the first, missing out on the second bout and narrowly winning a further two bouts.

It occurred to me during the opening bouts that our opposition were well turned out and trained. It wasn't going to be a walk over for our youngsters, but Jacky's calming instructions did have, as usual, a huge influence on the outcome of many of the fights.

The midway break arrived and four successful juniors paraded around our changing room with the confidence of accomplishment, proudly showing off their variety of prizes. However, it only served to escalate the tension for the remaining two young boxers.

Prizes, donated via sponsors, were on offer for each bout and generally consisted of cut-glass dishes, mantle clocks, tea and dinner services, silver candlesticks, and ornate figurines. The winner had first choice, and the more senior the boxer, the more valuable the prize.

My prizes over the years had over-filled all the available cupboard space at home. It was after Mum had opened one of the cupboard doors, whilst looking for a salad bowl, that a large three-tier china cake stand had crashed to the floor.

My dad made and erected new shelves down in the coal cellar of our terraced home after that disaster. These additional shelves had rapidly filled up with prizes, especially now that Alan was also adding to the collection.

Cups and shields that are presented to today's athletes would have been easier to stack and store.

As a matter of information, tragedy struck during a severe cold winter spell. Regrettably the adverse temperatures resulted in a burst water pipe flooding our cellar overnight, almost up to the top step (kitchen floor height). The

Rotherham Fire Brigade were on hand to pump out the water one Saturday afternoon.

We lost shelves full of photos and prizes in one fell swoop. Although I did manage to salvage, and still have, a set of repoussé silver salad servers from a magnificent large heavy-cut-glass salad bowl.

My first-ever prize, from Southey Green Working Men's Club in Sheffield, was a red leather writing case with pen, pencil and paper that I still use today. Sadly, not one boxing photo survived the flood.

However, I digress.

The second half got underway and the first of our remaining fighters, Eric, a young welterweight, was first up, losing on a points decision. He put in a good performance and the decision could have gone either way. He was followed by Simon, a very talented young middleweight, but I wasn't able to watch as it was my turn to get changed and prepare for my fight.

Jacky arrived at the door mouthing, 'Let's go.' A few minutes after escorting Simon back, I could tell that he had won by the expression on his face; his normally demure personality beamed with pride.

'Well done, Simon,' I mouthed as I passed alongside him on the way to the door.

With Jimmy in front and Jacky, with those shovel-like hands on my shoulders, behind we headed down the avenue of seats towards the red corner. We were accompanied by a pretty boisterous reception from the parents and followers of our club, who were determined to out-shout the packed hall.

Climbing up the steps, I ducked into the full-size ring, which I guess must have been at least eighteen foot by eighteen foot. No wonder some of the earlier youngsters looked lost in that size ring. It was perfect for the regular professional boxing and occasional wrestling bouts that the hall regularly hosted. My ideal arena, plenty of room for my mobile boxing style.

As I carefully stepped into the enormous ring, I couldn't help but notice that the light grey canvas bore the ingrained stains, marks and scars of many a fight. Blood does take some shifting, and there was plenty of it.

Jacky, without showing any signs of emotion, stood on the wide apron outside the ring, observing the crowd like the seasoned pro he was. The calming, telepathic influence that he had perfected over the years oozed from him, as I stood waiting for my opponent to make his way through the cheering home crowd to the blue corner.

As usual, we were distinguishable by a coloured red or blue sash that was strategically wrapped around our waists and corresponded with the colour of the corner post padding – not the fact that I had bright ginger hair and my opponent's was black and closely cropped.

It was an impressive sight in the blue corner as Stevie Boy, who was reacting to his enthusiastic local crowd, climbed into the ring and immediately performed what looked like a ritual dance in an arc around his corner. Show-off! Or was it peacocking to hide his nerves?

He was covered in a black and silver dressing gown and what looked like the logos of a dozen sponsors brightly adorning the front and back, with the gown's hood covering his head. By contrast, I simply had a towel wrapped around my shoulders and, for the first time, my hands were covered in bright red eight-ounce boxing gloves, rather than the usual old-fashioned brown ones.

Once the announcements had been made by the MC, we were summoned into the centre of the ring. As we came together, I realised that my opponent was sporting the first signs of a beard, which emphasised our age gap.

The smartly dressed referee reeled off our fight rules and regulations, with a 'may the best man win' comment, after which he sent us back to our respective corners.

Hell's bells! What a sight as I turned my back to Jacky ready for the opening round. My opponent now stood facing me stripped of his dressing gown, displaying a physique I had only ever seen in magazines. He looked like a young version of Charles Atlas, only bigger!

Bulging muscles on top of bulging muscles, looking as though body-building and weightlifting were more his game than boxing. That more than adequately answered the question about his extra weight, despite our similar height. Muscle, and he had an abundance of that, does weigh much heavier than normal flesh.

I didn't have time to dwell as the bell sounded to get the first round underway. As expected, he was slow but also full of power, as I soon found out, blocking a powerful right-hander which almost took me off my feet.

Towards the middle of the round, I was beginning to feel like I had been hit by a bus. My arms and shoulders ached through blocking those almighty swings which were sending me sideways and backwards. His extra weight was a huge advantage to him.

Well before the round came to an end, I had managed to analyse his fighting prowess and had him totally weighed up, making the necessary adjustments to confidently win the round.

I had realised that there was a kind of double stutter before he was able get a punch away, which allowed me time, once I had cottoned on, to beat him to the punch every time and then step out of reach before he could unleash a punch.

It occurred to me that he was probably muscle-bound, which was making it easy for me to skip around him and punch at will. From then on, I was rarely on that spot when he finally delivered a punch.

I was happy with the outcome of this first round and, from Jacky's comments as I sat on the uncomfortable wooden stool discussing the recommendations for the second round, I had made the right diagnosis and adjustments.

A quick mouth swill deposited safely into the bucket with a thumbs-up from Jimmy. I had once completely missed the bucket during one of my early fights and sprayed him with a full mouthful! Sponged down and gum shield safely sucked in, I was ready to go for round two.

'Keep him just out of arm's length and move fast, in and out, use your boxing skills, Ray, but don't become complacent, he is dangerous,' said Jacky as I stood up from the stool preparing to leave our corner as the bell sounded for the second round.

Advancing towards the centre of the ring, I was held back by the referee as Stevie Boy was still sat on his stool being worked on.

There's always a tad more latitude in amateur boxing and a few seconds extra don't make that much difference at this stage. I was happy to wait, so long as the round wasn't cut short.

A couple of seconds later we came together into the centre of this enormous ring under instructions from the referee. I could see what the delay had been about: his right eye, plastered in Vaseline, was showing signs of damage from the relentless left jabs and hooks I had been scoring heavily with during the latter part of the first round.

He came out of his corner with obvious instructions to attack and hustle me as the second round got underway.

His tactics were best described as like a bull in a china shop. He came charging at me with powerful arms swinging in an attempt at laying me flat. Fortunately, he didn't possess the speed or skills that, if combined with the power he had, would have spelled curtains for me.

The size of the ring was also working in my favour. I was much quicker than he was, allowing me the freedom to dominate most of the rounds.

Hours of sparring with Danny had paved the way for me to deal with my opponent's power tonight. But, whilst I wasn't being hit, it was strength-sapping blocking those vicious swings if I didn't get out of reach fast enough.

Patience is a virtue, or so I am told. It certainly worked in this case as he rapidly began to tire and run out of steam as the round progressed. Time to step up the action and take advantage of his inactivity.

It quickly became like a training session back at the gym, knocking the hell out of the heavy bag that doesn't hit back: a one-way, one-sided minute of heavy punching without much retaliation.

Now it was his turn to cover up against a barrage of non-stop action with which I was scoring heavily. There are always gaps in what appears to be a solid defence.

The second round came to an end with the referee pulling me off Stevie Boy. I hadn't heard the bell, but as I turned away to head back to my corner, I could see more lumps had developed on his face.

I had purposely gone all out for his face; he hadn't even flinched when I had connected with a couple of heavy body shots that should have had him gasping. He had developed a six pack that was as solid as a barn door. I clearly wasn't doing any damage in that area.

'Perfect,' Jacky said as he made me sit on the stool that Jimmy had placed in my corner this time, proceeding to massage my red-looking forearms and shoulders. He was as much in tune to what I had gone through as I was.

'Same again for the last round and don't get caught! Keep on the move and then step it up and get it over with.'

How strange that a simple comment like that from Jacky triggered memories from something that Danny had said during the latter part of our sparring sessions together, just before he had left for Ireland. 'Ray, you don't get paid for overtime in this business. Get it over with as soon as you can and get out of that ring.'

From where I was sat, looking over Jacky's shoulder as he knelt in front of me massaging my arms, I could observe the frantic activity taking place in the blue corner. Stevie Boy's seconds were working on the swellings around his cheeks and right eye in an effort to have him ready for the last round.

I knew they must be realising that he couldn't win unless he could knock me out; they would be drilling that into him for the last round.

Guess what I should be expecting coming my way in round three.

I was ready for the inevitable onslaught in the final round, spending the best part of the first half a minute on the move, covering up and making him miss most of his powerful wild swings.

Oh hell, where did that one come from? A punch caught me under the left rib cage from an almighty low right-hand swing that I had completely missed, whilst getting partially trapped in a neutral corner, sending a shudder through my body.

My lower ribs felt like they were cracked and were giving me searing pain as I searched for a deep breath while trying not to show any tell-tale flinching.

For the first time in my boxing career, I felt vulnerably damaged and unable to get a good breath into my lungs without feeling the almighty sharp pain.

Fortunately for me, Stevie Boy obviously wasn't aware of the damage he had inflicted and was concentrating on trying desperately to knock me out. A barrage of punches to my head was much easier for me to deal with, as he sacrificed any form of defence in his attempt at landing a KO punch.

I was trapped in that neutral corner for what seemed an eternity, desperately trying to refill my lungs with fresh air.

Through sheer desperation, my opponent, who was on a mission, was working like all hell was breaking loose, intent on not allowing me to escape, punching at me in a panic-like frenzy to bring the fight to an end.

Had he seen any facial reaction from me that indicated I was in trouble? I was still struggling to get a good breath into my lungs but doing my best to remain calm and using reaction speed to evade his onslaught.

I could see the frustration on my opponent's face as I ducked and weaved, using years of hard-learned skills to avoid his barrage of punches, making him miss and tire himself out.

Reaction speed can be learned and honed, and obviously extreme fitness plays a massive part. Having spent hours with my back to a wall in the gym or backed onto the ropes, hands by my side, avoiding head punches from a mixture of young boxers by using just the slightest of sideways or forward movement, really does quicken you up.

It didn't take long before he was blowing out of his backside again and now he was the one fighting to get his breath.

It was time to take back the initiative, as I had now partially recovered and able to breathe fairly comfortably without severe pain.

Spinning him round into the same corner, I set about delivering a bombardment of punches which he was unable to deal with.

I was now fully in control as he tried to cover up for around half a minute of relentless well-aimed punching that opened up a long cut just above his right eye which was soon bleeding profusely.

The referee, who was hovering close to the right side of me, was left with no option as he stepped between us and, grabbing my right arm, stopped the fight. As he pointed, for me to head to a neutral corner, he began to escort Stevie Boy back to his corner.

His team were quick to jump into the ring. They immediately took over from the referee and escorted him back to his corner. Whilst they worked on him for what seemed an eternity, I was able to evaluate my own damaged rib problem as I stood watching the frantic activities in my opponent's corner.

Although I had almost forgotten and hadn't felt any severe

pain for some time during my final attack, I was relieved to discover there was no real damage as I was able, using my thumb, to press around the area without any sharp pain.

A big sigh of relief. Sore but fortunately no cracked ribs.

The referee walked over and pointed for me to return to my corner and advised that the fight was definitely over.

Although I hadn't seen the fight doctor arrive, he had and had made the decision within seconds of inspecting the damage. For my part, I was pleased that the right decision had been made. I had observed the damage close up after a solid left hook had connected and it was one of the worst cuts I had ever seen.

Even without the doctor's decision, it would have been far too dangerous for him to continue. I didn't relish having to continue and be responsible for untold further damage.

We were eventually invited to come together in the middle of the ring either side of the referee where I could see, close up, the damaged eye which was still weeping through the heavily Vaselined covering.

After the result announcement had been made, Stevie Boy turned to me and grabbed my gloved left hand, raising my arm to the crowd. In a Geordie accent that I have come to love over the years, he said, 'Wow, that was one hell of a fight,' and shook my hand like we were best mates.

As we walked to his corner, I asked him if he was OK, lifting the middle rope for him to exit the ring after shaking hands with his corner men. He replied that he was fine and couldn't feel any pain. 'That will soon change, my new friend,' I thought, 'once the adrenaline has dispersed.'

I found out later that the fight doctor had put a few stitches in his cut eyebrow before he left for home, because Stevie Boy insisted that he wasn't visiting the local hospital to be treated. He would probably bear that scar for the rest of his life.

I have often stated that I was probably not the best fighter in the country at my weight, but I was certainly the fittest. That distinction more often than not made the difference between losing and winning.

So, in conclusion, if there's anyone out there that's as fit as I was, and possesses greater skills than I had, woe betide his or her opponents.

After arriving back at the hotel, with most of the parents, supporters and, of course, our successful boxing team in great spirits with seven out of nine winners, we were treated to one of the best late evening buffets I have ever had. It was presented on a twelve-foot-long table, full of the sort of food that I had only read about or seen in glossy magazines.

The Phoenix Boxing Club was being well and truly looked after.

Champagne had been flowing freely among the adults and, because the bottles weren't very well policed, after a round of celebrations I was able to sneak enough for me to get a real liking for the bubbly drink.

I didn't know what all the big fuss was about. It tasted just like fizzy lemonade to me, but I suddenly realised that it does do things to your head and legs.

I managed to crawl into bed around two in the morning, after I finally found the floor my room was on, never mind the room I was staying in, and slept like a baby.

Early morning breakfast had been organised, but by the time I had made it down to the dining room most of our group had finished breakfast and were heading back to their rooms to pack and get ready to board the bus. My bag was already packed, which gave me time to fill my belly with the food that was on offer.

We boarded the coach around 10am and, after the inevitable head count, set off for home with a boisterous happy group of fighters and parents. The coach was buzzing.

Back home I faced the usual questions about the entire weekend's adventure from my own family. This time, I was able to show the bruises that had materialised on my arms that had withstood the hammering, as well as the blueish area around my left ribs which were still a little tender to touch.

I was beginning to feel more optimistic and hopeful that, having moved up from a comfortable bantamweight to featherweight, it may open up the field and provide new opponents. That would see me through until it was time to decide between becoming a professional fighter for a living or staying at Steel, Peech and Tozer. By then, I was on a fantastic wage in the cogging mill, bringing in more than my dad was earning as a welder at the time.

The autopsy of the Newcastle fight was discussed during the following week's training. It was unanimously agreed that I had made the right diagnostics and had executed the correct adjustments early in the first round, which, in this case, made the difference between getting hurt and winning. The results of which are still stored in my memory bank, available when needed for the future. Perhaps that's the reason I can vividly recall most of my fights.

A few weeks later, after a steady Tuesday evening's training night, I was in a big rush to get home to watch the monthly boxing tournament on our new telly.

The BBC was televising an international amateur boxing tournament that England ABA were competing in. As part of a series, England would compete against a different country each month for the next six months. That evening England were up against the hosts, Poland.

I settled down, with a mug of tea, on our old threadbare three-seater couch in front of a roaring open coal fire in the kitchen, joined by Alan and Dad. David sat at my feet on the newly handmade pegged rug.

Curtains had been closed and lights out to get the best visual experience from our new-fangled black and white twelve-inch television. We had a handful of shilling coins at the ready to feed the meter, which would ensure an uninterrupted couple of hours of viewing.

Our new TV, rented on contract from Wigfall's store, operated on a shilling slot system that would be emptied once a month by the Wigfall man. After the agreed monthly contract was taken out, whatever excess coins the box contained would then be returned to us so that we could feed the hungry slot again for further viewing. As I recall, a shilling became increasingly more difficult to get hold of as collection time neared but then was found in abundance after meter collection had taken place in our area. The shortage didn't seem to last very long.

As we were later to find out, watching sport on black and white telly wasn't going to be easy. One of my fond memories is that of when the snooker commentator Ted Lowe advised the nation, 'For those of you who are watching in black and white, the pink is next to the green!'

I digress!

The opening credits displayed a short film which provided a collage of many English representative fighters, together with an explanation of the background to the night's match.

Exciting commentary from a very knowledgeable commentator gave these events a special feel.

The tournament kicked off with a middleweight bout and representing England was a fighter I had seen fighting on the same bill, on many occasions, up and down the country.

A great boxing display and a first win for England, quickly followed by a light heavyweight contest that didn't go the distance, resulting in another win, this time in the form of a last-round KO for the English fighter.

It seemed strange to see some of the heavier fighters turning out before the flyweights during those international fights. Usually, the lightweight fighters start the proceedings, progressing to the heavy guys bringing up the rear, so to speak. I loved watching the mix of weights and talented fighters, no matter which country they may be from, although patriotically we were rooting and cheering every English win.

The next bout at welterweight was a real treat to watch, with Poland taking the win.

What I wasn't ready for was the next England representative!

Surprise to start with, then shock, despair, despondency and sick to the stomach all in one go. All words that would never adequately describe how I felt at that moment when the camera zoomed in to the face of England's next representative.

My world had just been turned upside down with utter frustration.

'Whatever is the matter?' asked Dad, as I jumped up and yelled, 'What?!'

I pointed at the screen and screamed in anger at the telly. 'That's Sammy, my opponent from Liverpool,' I yelled.

What was he doing fighting for England? I'd always

assumed the best fighters would be the choice for the national team, so why him and not me? I half screamed, yelling at the screen and suddenly realising that my dad had grabbed my arm rather forcefully.

'Calm down, sit down and let's watch his performance,' he said.

The next ten minutes were difficult to watch. I was fuming, unable to control my emotions, which were all over the place. I am not at all proud to say I honestly willed, in silence, for Sammy's opponent to batter the living daylights out of him. That's really not my style.

I felt a sense of guilt for my thoughts; I really shouldn't be blaming Sammy.

Although I had been hoping for the English fighter to lose, he did actually win convincingly on points, which added further to my frustration.

You may recall me mentioning that, even though the Phoenix Boxing Club had seven or eight ABA champions, not one of us had been called to represent our country; South Yorkshire just didn't seem to exist.

The impact of that one incident had a deeply profound effect on me. That was a blow, well below the belt, making me question my own sense of values that I had long since associated with the Amateur Boxing Association and British boxing.

I couldn't comprehend; everything I had ever been taught and upheld since starting out on my boxing career had taken a severe battering. In one fell swoop, I had fallen out of love with the boxing establishment.

I was deeply hurt. Moral integrity was now in question of an association which I had been proud to have been part of.

'If that's what the ABA stands for then I want nothing more to do with boxing. That's me done,' I venomously declared with passion to both Alan and my dad, and I meant it. It had become a matter of principle and honour which I was finding difficult to come to terms with.

After sitting down with both Mum and Dad later that evening, when my brothers had gone to bed, Dad suggested that I take time out and stay away from boxing for a couple of weeks. That would give me time before making any rash, hasty decisions that would impact on the rest of my life. I agreed but knew deep down that, no matter what anyone said, I wouldn't change my mind.

What had been done that evening couldn't be undone.

Out of a sense of duty and respect, a couple of weeks later I walked down to the gym and, with a heavy heart, talked to Jacky about my decision. He was shocked to say the least. I was emotionally in tatters and struggled to get my reasons into understandable sentences.

Jacky understood my frustration, agreeing with my not-so-eloquent synopsis. But after a feeble attempt at trying to change my mind, we shook hands for the very last time.

I walked out of the gym without uttering another word to anyone and was physically sick in the gutter on Sheffield Road, less than ten feet from the gym doors.

I was in tatters. My whole way of life and career had come to an abrupt end, just before I had reached my seventeenth birthday.

I do believe that Jacky thought I would get over it and return to the fold in due course. But the values and disciplines that had been instilled in me over the last seven years were so deeply rooted, I was convinced that I couldn't change if I tried.

It's strange, when I think back, how I was able to come to terms with not training like a professional boxer over the following few months. A strange new way of life!

But life has to carry on and, fortunately, football had come to the rescue and kept me sane, providing me with the necessary adrenaline fix I thought I could do without. I was playing with the firm's team in the county senior league and enjoying the new challenge.

Around six months later, a letter asking me to contact social services was attached to my clock card, which revealed that Jack Solomons had been in touch with the club asking for my address. I declined the offer.

I have thought long and hard over the years about that Tuesday evening and the outcome of that experience. What if we didn't have a TV and I hadn't seen Sammy representing England? There is probably no other way that I would have found out. Who knows where my path would have taken me? Would I have become a professional fighter?

Obviously my life would have been very different if that had been the case, but I stand by the decision I made that evening and I can honestly say that I wouldn't change how my life has panned out.

I will always be eternally grateful to both Benny Kemp and Jacky Pearson, who are both sadly long gone.

For as long as I am still alive, they will live on in my mind and continue to be a source of inspiration whenever I need guidance and encouragement when taking on a seemly impossible challenge. I still hear their voices in times of need and draw positivity.

Because the values that I was taught in those early years had become so influential and the banner under which I lived my life, they have continued to be the standard for the rest of my life. There's no going back, only forward, taking great memories into the rest of my life.

Should I bury this period in a time capsule for posterity now the story has finally been told?

12

Don't mess with a little old lady from Dalton

Life instantly became much easier after the French weekend trip as I settled down into a more stable and steady daily routine of eating, sleeping, managing the old muscles and tendons, and running. Lots of running.

Did I mention running?

I do believe that the marathon team had, by that time, started to breathe a collective sigh of relief. We were on the home straight!

I was excited that all the plans for the very last marathon, which would finish with me running into Newman School, had been sorted during a short meeting at the school, halfway through one of the marathons.

A large colourful banner had suddenly appeared shortly afterwards, highlighting the final plans with an open invitation for everyone to come to the school and celebrate my final run-in on Wednesday 14th September. The banner was proudly displayed right across the front of the school and clearly visible from the very busy dual carriageway.

Day after day the miles continued to stack up and the old body kept moving forward one foot in front of the other. But unfortunately, the income wasn't keeping up with the effort that was being applied, which kept a negative cloud hanging over me. However, when mentioning my concern, it was implied that, as the event was drawing to a conclusion, the media attention would greatly increase and send the fundraising through the roof. Ah well, as a complete newbie to this fundraising malarkey, who was I to question that?

Before long, the day arrived when I was able to count on just two hands the number of marathons left. Time seemed to be just flying by all of a sudden.

As the countdown began and the media coverage increased, the contributions started to gain momentum again and for that I will be forever grateful. It brings to mind an incident during one of the later marathons that had me in hysterics.

It was late afternoon and I was running through Dalton on the outskirts of Rotherham, on my way home from a meeting at the gym, when I became conscious of this small blue car that was alongside me. When I looked inside, I could see a little old lady frantically waving her hands at me. I waved back in acknowledgement, then she suddenly shot off, coming to a stop in the middle of the road a few yards further on, and got out.

'You're him!' she said. 'You're him, aren't you?' she cried excitedly as I arrived alongside her. 'I said to my husband, "That's him, that's the marathon man," when you ran past our house. We've just been watching you on telly.'

By then the traffic was building back up the road, with drivers honking their horns in displeasure at being held up behind her car.

We quickly established that I was indeed who she thought I was. She opened her handbag that she was clutching and handed me a fiver from her purse.

'It's great what you're doing for them kids,' she said. Then, with a look that said, 'Don't mess with me, young man,' she put two fingers up to the first driver behind her, slowly got back into her car and disappeared up the road.

I was in stitches as I ran the next five miles home. Never mess with a little old lady from Dalton!

'It's about the kids now more than ever,' I thought as I carried on home.

As the days passed, it soon became a single-figure count. Wow, just a paltry five marathons to go. I could crawl them if needed.

The winning post was so very close and the excitement was beginning to build. But keeping a lid on the eagerness to start the celebrations needed much mental discipline; that day would come soon enough.

Luckily I had another marathon coming up that I had been so looking forward to.

The seventy-first turned out to be an amazing marathon that's hard to put into words. But proud, satisfying and emotional would be high on the list for starters.

The sponsor, Handmade Burger Co, whose head office was situated just out of the centre of Birmingham, had made the commitment some time ago. My eldest grandson, Adam, area manager for the company, had made the owners and management team aware of my challenge. They had agreed and had actually sponsored two of the marathons.

I'd arranged to run the seventy-first marathon in and around Birmingham and had agreed to finish it at their flagship restaurant, just off the famous Bull Ring in the centre of the city.

Adam, during one of our telephone chats, casually announced that he would be running with me.

I remember telling Adam that, even though his comment hadn't surprised me, there wasn't anywhere near enough time for him to put the training in for such a long-distance run. Undeterred, he unsurprisingly wasn't to be dissuaded – he's got the Matthews blood, after all. 'I will be OK, Grandad. You're running seventy-five marathons, I can at least run one,' he said.

'Well, in that case you had better get started. Put some miles in and get as running fit as possible,' I had said to him during our telephone conversation.

I was seriously concerned that, while he'd excelled in many sports, Adam had never run much above a 10K in his life. Although he is a fit lad, running long distances was not covered in his sporting achievements. He, however, has never been one to turn down a challenge.

I was determined to make that marathon a classic, having spent a good few hours on my laptop working out a suitable route that would see us finishing at the Handmade Burger restaurant in Birmingham city centre.

As the route began to take shape, I felt confident that it would be impossible to plot a flatter marathon.

The idea was that we would run the bulk of the marathon heading north on the Grand Union Canal.

If we were to start at one of their local restaurants in Solihull, we would probably need to add just an extra couple of miles on the canal before leaving for our run into the city.

Having completed the seventieth marathon shortly after 1pm on Friday afternoon, I packed a bag and, after saying goodbye to Maureen, drove down to Birmingham to set up the following day's marathon with Adam.

I had been invited down to their head office to meet Adam and the Handmade Burger management team. That had the added bonus of being able to leave my car, overnight, in the shared lock-up car park behind their office close to the centre of Birmingham.

After all the good-luck wishes and handshakes had been made, we left the office and Adam drove us both out of the city to a local Solihull hotel, close to the following day's starting point in the Touchwood shopping centre.

Charlotte, Adam's then-girlfriend who is now his wife, arrived to give him support and, after an early evening meal, we retired to our rooms.

Throughout the day, Adam had shown no signs of being concerned about what was in front of him. However, that didn't stop me from worrying throughout the night about the fitness he'd need to take on this huge challenge. I was awake long before the alarm was due to go off.

We met in the dining room and, during breakfast, I outlined the route we would be taking, which actually involved running south away from Birmingham for about four miles. We would then make an about-turn and head north on the towpath for a further nineteen miles, before leaving the Grand Union canal. Our aim was to run into Birmingham City Centre as close to 26.2 miles as I could make it.

After a few photos with the Handmade Burger staff, who had come into the restaurant early to give us a great send-off, Adam and I set out in the pouring rain from the Touchwood shopping centre, Solihull. This would be the longest run, by miles, for him.

We left the shopping complex heading south into the lashing rain and, after a couple of miles, were running through what can only be described as the money belt of Birmingham. Some fantastic big expensive houses with cars on the drives to match.

By the time we reached the bridge, which never seemed to come, taking us over the Grand Union Canal, I was able to breathe a huge sigh of relief knowing that we were on the right track. I was running on just memory of the planned route.

After crossing the bridge, we finally made a left turn and headed north through a small village which suddenly revealed the entrance onto the rain sodden towpath on the eastern side of the canal.

We both looked like drowned rats by this point as we set foot on the towpath and headed due north, laughing at one another's dishevelled appearance but both in great spirits.

The early part of the canal path proved to be ankle deep in mud and water – even the ducks were swimming in the pools in front of us.

'No point in trying to avoid the puddles, Adam,' I remember saying. We might as well just go for it and continue in as straight a line as possible, using less energy than trying to jump over or veer around the pools of water. Much paddling and splashing like a couple of big kids followed for the next ten miles.

Mile after mile, we made steady progress. I was becoming more and more impressed with Adam's stamina and mental attitude and less and less concerned as he once again took over the lead on a narrowing section of the towpath. It's hard to believe that he had never even run a half marathon before this tough marathon challenge.

The canal around the north-eastern side of Birmingham proved to be a very interesting mix of dereliction in places but utilised and modernised in others, obviously having had a fortune spent to bring it up to date. Very impressive.

During our run up the canal and still some distance away from our Birmingham turn-off, it became apparent that there was another running event taking place as more and more runners came towards us holding maps and course instructions.

At around twenty miles into our marathon, we were made welcome and took full advantage of the event's drink station, topping up our water sacks and snacking on bananas and fruit cake. I even came away with a ten-pound note, a donation from one of the ladies after Adam had explained about our challenge and what we were up to.

Fantastic, especially when they didn't know me from Adam. Sorry, couldn't resist!

As we continued to make progress, I also met quite a few former running colleagues who were taking part in the race and were keen to congratulate me on my challenge. Adam was starting to think I knew everyone!

We finally left the Grand Union Canal towpath after returning, for the second time, passed the large Sea World centre building, adding the extra three miles we needed to make up the distance. It could have been soul-destroying passing the point of leaving the canal, only to run a further three miles overall before running back to this exit point, but Adam took it in his stride and made no sign of being affected.

With around one and a half miles to go, we headed over the canal footbridge and entered the pedestrian zone, taking a detour through the busy cordoned-off town centre which was mostly under renovation and new construction.

The edge of the city was buzzing with thousands of shoppers milling around the famous Bullring, which was undergoing a massive upgrade and was already starting to look amazing.

I was now following half a step behind Adam, who confidently steered us through the shoppers to our final destination, the Handmade Burger Co's flagship restaurant, which suddenly came into view.

We ran in to the entrance canopy to a rapturous reception from some of the management and staff and the very enthusiastic Charlotte.

A bottle of Champagne, a large box of chocolates and a bunch of flowers were presented to the prodigious grandson. He, without doubt, had put in a five-star performance throughout the five hours of running, without once giving me any real cause for concern. Neither had he made any complaints or asked that dreaded question, 'How much further is there to go?', which would have been a sure sign of distress, even though I knew he had been silently suffering with blisters on his feet.

A bottle of cold lager, delicious Handmade Burger, onion rings, chicken wings and chunky chips were on offer, which I wolfed down without touching the sides. Be rude not to and just what the doctor ordered to round off the seventy-first marathon.

Time to head back to pick up my car and head for home, after dropping Adam and Charlotte back at their hotel to finish the weekend off in Solihull and start his recovery.

I was on a great high at the end of a fantastic day and found it difficult to come down all the way home. How many grandads would ever get the chance to experience such a remarkable feeling that had been with me the whole day? I am so proud to have been able to share our amazing, demanding, character-building and challenging day together.

Adam, you're a star. It was an immense pleasure running a marathon with you.

*

Just four days of running stood between me and the finish line at Newman School.

The day after the Birmingham run I was back running around Maltby for a marathon sponsored by Dave Marsh at Universal Cycle Centre, a local shop with everything needed for cyclists. The day after that was the second of P Flannery Plant Hire Company's marathons which had been organised by Claire Pettinger, one of my friends who had taken part in the trip to France. Maltby Carpets & Beds-sponsored marathon would then follow. Martin Mitchell, the owner, had been a massive supporter of this challenge, not only giving financial help but also time spent in advertising our fundraising initiatives and providing raffle prizes.

*

The last day had finally arrived and "seventy-five" had finally evolved into an actual real number, not just a dream.

I awoke from a surprisingly good night's sleep to the full realisation that my marathon way of life, which I had honestly enjoyed, day after day, was about to become a thing of the past.

The long-established plan for the final marathon was for me to run locally during the day and steadily accumulate around nineteen miles in safety mode before making my way down to Herringthorpe Stadium for around 4pm. This would leave me with just half an hour and two miles to run, with a group of friends, from the stadium into Newman School.

The weather, like an omen for how the day would pan out, was just perfect for running and all had gone well during the day. Fortunately, I had given myself plenty of time as I slowly racked up the miles around Maltby, continually being stopped by locals wanting autographs, selfies or just to wish me well. Most were aware of this final marathon that had been highly publicised over the past couple of weeks.

After a bite to eat, I set back off running down to the stadium, where a crowd of excited friends was waiting for me as I arrived at the car park. The crowd included David Thompson, one of the New Balance welcoming committee members whom I had met in Birchwood, Warrington. He was accompanied by a van full of water and freebies for my group of friends.

Checking the distance on my watch revealed that I had a little under three miles to complete the last marathon distance.

I headed for the track, to where it had all begun almost eleven weeks previous, to run with a few supporters, strangely enough, just one mile around the track. How amazing!

The moment finally arrived for me to set off for the very last time, but these final couple of miles would prove to be dramatically different and another of the more memorable occasions in the old memory archives.

Rachel Pawson, director of Pawson Transport, had arrived in one of their massive Scania trucks to provide an escort for my run into the school grounds. Stood in the car park with all lights blazing and flashing like Blackpool illuminations, this truck would provide me with an amazing escort with a difference.

I remember feeling like a real-life celebrity and thinking to myself as we set off, most celebrities would be provided with a police escort, even a cycle escort would have been great. But hell's bells! Nobody but me could end up with a massive truck escort. It must have been visible to everyone, towering above us as we left the stadium and headed out on the public highway for that last couple of miles to Newman School.

I remember looking back, whilst running down Broom Lane, wondering how much disruption we were causing to the normal day-to-day traffic. We were taking up most of the road.

The traffic stretched back as far as I could see, although the drivers seemed happy enough to accept being held up and patiently followed us down to the traffic island a quarter of a mile away. Perhaps they were all aware of this final event; there had been loads of local publicity over the last few weeks.

I had made arrangements earlier in the day to ring through to BBC Look North's Nicola Rees and let her know as soon as we arrived at the top of the hill above the school. She would be waiting in the school grounds and would pass on the news, letting everyone know that we were on schedule and running according to plan.

'I am on my way up to you, don't set off yet,' she said. That was OK with me, we were a little early anyway.

A minute later I was all wired up for sound. Nicola had fitted me up with the standard BBC remote microphone which was now attached to the front of my vest and the receiver clipped to the back of my shorts.

'It will save time before we do the interview,' she said, before disappearing back down the road in her little Mini.

I was determined to keep my promise of running into Newman School at bang on 4:30pm and couldn't take my eyes off my watch. That small computer window on my wrist flashed up that I had completed just over 26.2 miles already.

Nervously conscious of the pre-arranged schedule, time slowly ticked on.

'It's time to go, guys,' I excitedly announced to my escort and friends. At exactly 4:28pm on Wednesday 14th September 2016, we set off down the short hill to Newman School around two hundred yards away.

I was tingling all over as I put my legs in gear and made my way down the road to the sound of stirring music that had suddenly erupted from the grounds of Newman School. It was 'Chariots of Fire', if I remember rightly.

The nearer we got, the louder the music became. As we entered the school grounds, I became acutely aware that my heart was thumping louder in my chest, even louder than the music. For the first time the huge crowd of children at the front of the school became visible.

The children were strategically sat cheering beneath the raised colourful banners in front of the school building that had obviously been made by the school to welcome me.

There's nothing complex about how I was feeling at the sight of all the children as they came into view. Just pure raw emotions which had been building up over the last few days and were so very close to erupting and taking over, if I couldn't get a grip. I hadn't envisaged the level of emotion that I was feeling.

I had run through the gates, onto the field and around the cordoned-off route with my running escort following just a couple of steps behind. As I headed towards the large inflatable archway at the finish line, I could see the final ribbon, which would mark the end of my marathon challenge, being tightly held by a couple of the young Newman School students.

The large, jubilant crowd was cheering, waving banners and waiting to greet me.

'You've got to hold it together, Ray. Come on, this is what it's all been about,' I kept thinking to myself as I took stock of the enormity of the occasion.

The joy and happiness became almost overpowering as the whole field had suddenly come to life with students running to get the best views, while TV cameramen and photographers stood capturing the final run in.

I inadvertently ran into the arms of Lyndsay Pitchley, our mayor at the time, who was stood cheering just behind the finish line, nearly bowling her over before coming to a complete standstill.

You can stop now, Ray, I almost shouted out. The running's over.

First port of call as soon as I had run through the finish line was to give thanks to the Newman School gang as I walked along the long line of children, teachers and parents. They were all closely packed together, four or five deep, and had been patiently waiting to provide the amazing welcome I was receiving.

Drums were still being loudly banged, but the cheers from the children seemed to drown them out. Just incredible, more amazing than I could have ever imagined.

Once again, I came close to losing it big-style as I stood facing the kids. All the emotions welled up and that time a tear or two did pop out.

Even as I write and re-live this part of the event, I am conscious of a sharp rise in my heart rate.

I gulped and swallowed the urge to just let the pent-up emotions go. Fortunately, I spotted my safe harbour, Maureen, who had been stood in front of the welcoming children waiting for my arrival with my daughter Karen, granddaughter Holly and sister-in-law Barbara. I gave my wife the biggest hug while I composed myself.

They were all here to greet me. Gulp. It was like nothing I'd ever experienced before.

Thankfully the spotlight had suddenly been transferred across to Maureen, who was being presented with a large bunch of flowers and a framed signed thank-you document from the children. Catherine, the school's deputy headteacher, said, as she handed the flowers over, that they were 'in recognition of your support over all these years'. I used that time to pull myself back together again.

How does anyone prepare themselves for an emotional roller coaster such as that? Even though I should have been more prepared for the inevitable accolades and kind but flattering words, it certainly came as a shock to the system. Surely, that level of sentiment is not something that anyone can be taught to deal with.

Time for speeches from the headteacher, Julie Mott, as

I worked my way back along the crowd to where the main delegation was waiting. Julie spoke about my extraordinary challenge and what the money raised would mean for the children. Embarrassing, but an extremely proud moment as I stood listening to her comments. Tragically, Julie passed away without seeing the fruits of this challenge come to fruition.

The late GMB trade unionist Eric Batty followed Julie and, during another tear-jerking speech, I was presented with a large silver platter commemorating the success of my challenge. GMB had totally embraced my challenge, sponsoring the first and last of the marathons, with Eric playing a major role in the presentation of this lasting memory.

TV interviews that had been set up by my acting publicist, Sean, followed in an extremely orderly fashion, which saved me the hassle of having to decide who to talk to next.

Nicola headed up the queue and, whilst I declined her offer of being whisked off up the M1 to the Leeds Look North studios, we agreed to do a later live link interview which would go out during that evening's main news programme at around 6:45pm.

Before then I had my first-ever interview with Adam Fowler, a reporter for ITV Calendar News. Adam put me at ease right from the start, leading me through the interview and asking all the right questions to bring out the full story that I felt had made me look like an achiever.

I found Adam easy to talk to and got the feeling that the end result that would be shown later that evening would no doubt get the message across that, although the marathons had been completed, the rest of my challenge was yet to be fulfilled. I was still looking to raise the seventy-five thousand pounds I had set out to achieve.

Sheffield Live TV followed with another cracking

interview and then Radio Sheffield, as well as a number of media reporters and photographers, including Dave Poucher from the Rotherham Advertiser and then Rich Sales from Newman School for their archives.

After mingling with parents, friends and supporters for an hour or so, soaking up the occasion, the final TV interview was set up. This time it was a live recording as Nicola relayed all of the day's activities back to the Look North studio, where the evening news programme was being presented by Harry Gration and Leanne Brown.

Outlining the enormity of what I had achieved, the interview also highlighted what the challenge had been all about. The thousands of miles that I had run over the past eleven weeks had raised enough money to provide Newman School with new wheelchair swings, roundabouts and a soft rubber playground for the children to run around in safety.

After a short speech thanking everyone and paying my respects to the children, who had been so patient throughout the past three hours, for an amazing end to an incredible journey, it was time to make our exit.

But the day wasn't quite over. It was time to head over to New York Stadium, the home of Rotherham United FC, for an event that had been organised some time ago. At the ground, I was to be introduced to the crowd during the home match against Nottingham Forest, in the hope of raising some further donations.

I said goodbye to Maureen and my family; Karen would be dropping her off on her way back home to Worksop.

Sean, who had overseen all the media arrangements during the day, walked me down to his car, which was parked up on the grass at the bottom of the field, and casually mentioned that I was to be presented with the British Citizen Award. I almost didn't hear what he had just told me as my mind was understandably elsewhere.

'We are not allowed to tell anyone yet as they have imposed a press embargo on the announcement until we are cleared to go live,' he said.

It turned out that, unbeknown to me, my friend David Greenfield, who had been tucked away in the crowd at Newman School, had nominated me for the award some time ago. However, the timing of the announcement couldn't have been more incredible.

I now have letters after my name, you know!

The short journey down to the stadium gave me time to reflect and take stock of what the day had clearly meant, not only to me but the hundreds of friends who had played an enormous part in the proceedings.

We were met at the stadium by Jamie Noble, head of the Rotherham United Community Sports Trust, who invited us onto the magnificent pitch. I was eventually introduced to the crowd after they had managed to get the stadium microphone system working. Photos with some of the team, followed with a promise of raising funds during the match, brought our visit to an end.

Rotherham beat Nottingham Forest, by the way.

Time to finally head home and bring one of my greatest sporting achievements to a close. I felt spent and drained of all emotion, as we silently made our way home.

As I walked through the door just after 8pm, Maureen and I just looked at one another and laughed.

What a roller coaster of a day it had been. And now it was all done.

The Path to Success

*

Guest Contribution

Adam Dukes, my grandson

'Of course I will run a marathon with you, Grandad.' A sentence I never thought I'd say, not least to my seventy-four-year-old grandad.

Did I honestly think he would manage all seventy-five and that I'd actually have to run when it came down to it? There is a reason I said I would run the seventy-first and not the first!

As I heard of him running his fiftieth run in France, the realisation that I had just twenty-one days to train to run a marathon hit home hard. The thought of running a marathon seems like a huge feat to most. But when your grandad is running seventy-five of them consecutively, to be able to manage just one all of a sudden seemed a really different accomplishment, a mindset I was very thankful to be able to maintain.

So, after three training runs, three miles, nine miles and finally a fifteen-mile run, the day of marathon seventy-one arrived. It came around quickly, far too quickly for my liking, but I was ready as I was ever going to be. I'm not one to shy away from a challenge, but not only was I about to run a marathon with little to no training, it was also absolutely bucketing down with rain.

Very quickly after leaving Solihull, we hit the Grand Union Canal and the rain was coming down hard. Where once was a lovely footpath, puddles of water were forming fast, and very quickly we all but gave up trying to find 'dry land' for our feet. We realised that we were having difficulty knowing where the canal finished and the path started, giving extra danger to every step, forever wondering if there was ground underfoot and sure that one of us would shortly be having a swim.

After about eight miles, our feet were soaked through. It felt like I was running on glass. With a long way to go, this was worrying for me and certainly uncharted territory However, when I looked to my side and saw the smile on Grandad's face, the pain just seemed to disappear. I had been concentrating so much on the fact I needed to finish I'd totally forgot to enjoy the experience. When would I ever get the chance to run like this with my grandad?

How far would I have made it past that breaking point without that moment? Thankfully I will never have to find out!

With pain in my feet and completely soaked, I was determined to keep going and finish the run. My own pride wasn't going to let me, not when your grandad's getting close to having already run two thousand miles.

As we neared the end of the run and made our way into the city centre, the run became easier as I knew where I was and that the end wasn't far away. We made it to the finish line and I was completely and utterly exhausted. We arrived to a fanfare where I was struggling to catch my breath from slowing down and could barely stand. Whereas Grandad necked a bottle of beer and had a chat with everyone! A very stark contrast. I removed my trainers and stood with my hot feet on the cold pavement and could physically see the steam rising from the floor! I was so ready to lie down and Grandad still had four more marathons to go.

The experience is really beyond anything I could explain. Not only was it demanding on my body, but it was an experience with my grandad that I will never forget. I am grateful to him for having me by his side while he achieved something so monumental. It is a memory that I'll hold forever and when he's telling everyone of his achievement, I too can say, 'I ran a marathon!' Whilst I may not have, and don't intend to, run seventy-five marathons in my lifetime, let alone in as many days, I am so proud of what my grandad has accomplished. I don't know anyone else with his sense of drive and motivation to help others.

*

Guest Contribution

Adam Fowler, ITV reporter

I was in a bit of a daze when I first met Adam Fowler, shell-shocked is probably the right phrase, during the awesome reception I received during the final marathon in the grounds of Newman School. But, like the true professional he is, I was put at ease and guided through our first interview. Adam is always on my wavelength during our interviews and continues to get the message across. Invaluable. Thank you for your continued support, my friend.

Ray Matthews

It was a glorious September day, back in 2016, when I first met Ray. We'd already featured him a few times on ITV Calendar as he made his way through his gruelling challenge: seventy-five marathons in seventy-five days.

The news desk sent me to Newman School in Rotherham to catch up with Ray as he crossed the finish line in front of a huge crowd of family, friends and supporters.

Eventually Ray appeared to a huge roar of approval as the crowds cheered him over the line. It had been a long journey to the end, he told me: 'It never seemed as though it was coming then all of a sudden it's here like an express train. Just fantastic... I never dreamt it was going to be this good.'

I asked him if he'd ever had any doubts about whether he'd complete the challenge.

'No, never. Never. This is a challenge I always knew I could do. For me, the biggest challenge is what I'm trying to do for the school. And that is raising this enormous amount of money.'

I asked Ray if he fancied doing seventy-six marathons when he turned seventy-six. He declined, saying he might wait until he was a hundred and do a hundred then. I'm sure he was joking but I wouldn't put it past him!

A year later, I was back at Newman School but this time it was to see the fruits of Ray's labours. Ray had raised £35,000 and persuaded two local building firms to build a play area and a pathway running around the school. It would mean parts were accessible to children that they hadn't been able to explore before. The children clearly adored Ray and he felt the same way. 'They've become part of Team Ray,' he told us.

Only a month later I found myself back at Newman School once again. That time, though, instead of Ray presenting something to the children, it was me presenting something to Ray. He'd been put forward as ITV Calendar's 'fundraiser of the year'. He was invited, along with other regional ITV winners, to attend the Daily Mirror Pride of Britain Awards, televised annually on ITV.

Despite some deserving competition, a panel of judges voted Ray to be the winner.

I was delighted to be able to surprise Ray with the award, and although he was gobsmacked he was very quick to pay tribute to the other nominees who had missed out, which I thought was typically humble of Ray.

Often, that would be the end of the story. We'd covered Ray's incredible feat, what had been done with the money he raised and now here we were, presenting him with an award from the viewers to mark his achievement. But Ray always has something up his sleeve.

So it was in May 2018 that I was back with Ray again, this time in the middle of Rotherham. He'd only gone and set up the town's first 10k, raising money for Age UK Rotherham.

'A few years ago, I had a dream about putting a town centre race on. I've run marathons all over the world and I know what it feels like when you're running through a town when people are shouting your name… it really does lift athletes. So the idea was years ago that we'd put on a Rotherham town centre race, so my dream is coming true,' he said at the time.

It didn't stop there: Ray was also launching a campaign to get school kids to run a mile a day, to improve fitness and help concentration. So a few days later we found ourselves at St Bede's Catholic School as hundreds of children raced around in front of the cameras. Interviewing a few of them it was clear that Ray's original seventy-five marathon challenge remained an inspiration, even though it was nearly two years ago at this point.

In February 2020, the phone rang again. According to Age

UK, more than a million older people go more than a month without speaking to a friend, neighbour or family member.

So Ray had given himself a new challenge: to tackle loneliness in old age. He'd been touring around local cafes and libraries, talking to the elderly about the opportunities presented by retirement. I met up with him for ITV Calendar at Maltby Library.

'The message I'm trying to get over,' he told me, 'is retirement is not the end of the world – it's the beginning. You now have the time to devote to everything you feel like you've wanted to do.'

Ray's living proof of that, so you can't say he doesn't practise what he preaches! As I write this it's nearly five years since I chased Ray over the finish line at Newman School and I'm arranging to meet up with him again. Ray turns eighty in June 2021 and is getting eighty schools to get eighty pupils running a mile each, to raise eighty pounds per school for the 80-80-80 challenge.

The last five years have seen Ray achieve so much, from improving Newman School, introducing the first Rotherham town centre 10K, to getting the very young to go for a morning run to getting the very old out and about too. I once signed off a report by saying I look forward to seeing what Ray does next because he always surprises us. That was true then and it's true now. Well done, Ray!

13

Fulfilling my promise to Newman School

Well then, my friend, now you know when, how and why my boxing career ended. Hands up those of you who thought I would be knocked out and end up hospitalised?

You have also seen me cross the finishing line of the seventy-fifth marathon and, be honest, who thought I would never make it to the end?

Not much more to say then about that side of the challenge unless, of course, you are curious to know whether I was able to deliver on my promise to the children at Newman School?

You are? Great! Well, in that case, read on.

*

A short while after the final marathon had been completed, we discovered that we had in fact raised a magnificent £35,000. Splendid indeed, as fundraising goes, but disappointingly nowhere near enough to pay for the works I'd promised the school. So what in heaven's name would I have to do if running seventy-five marathons wasn't enough?

As time passed, it became evident that I was never going to reach the financial target that we needed. This, as you will recall, was to construct the path, the major part of my challenge, as well as providing the soft surface and equipment for the Newman School children.

It was during a visit to discuss the handover of the funds to the school team that I was extremely fortunate to be introduced to Leigh Garbutt. Leigh was head of customer experience at Fortem (formerly Willmott Dixon) and was visiting the school to finalise plans for a construction project that was in the pipeline.

During our meeting I mentioned about my dream, and what I was trying to achieve for the children.

We visited the area of the school that had been ear-marked for the modifications and playground equipment, and as we strolled around the lower playground, the idea of attracting a construction company to take on the path project materialised.

'Great idea, Ray,' I thought. If I couldn't provide the path via the monetary fundraising way, perhaps this second option would work?

When I broached the subject, Leigh appeared interested and receptive. Had fate played a hand that day? It really didn't matter how we got the path constructed, as long as we did it.

A few days later, I received a phone call from Tom Knight, a long-standing member of Rotherham Sitwell Rotary Club, who had been told about my challenge and what I was trying to achieve. He listened to my idea and offered to help.

During our first meeting together, it became evident that Tom was keen to get involved and introduced Bob Sutton, contracts manager at Eurovia Contracting, into the mix. His view was that this second company could greatly enhance the possibility of getting the path constructed.

A meeting of both companies to outline our plan and work out the viability of the merger proved to be a huge success. The format for working together was agreed, in principle, during a further meeting that Tom had arranged.

Eurovia would supply plant and equipment and Fortem act as the project management team and support.

By this time, Tom had drawn up detailed plans, plotting every substantial tree, outlining the meandering route through the dense shrubbery, woodland and around the large field at the front of the school. The path would end at the playground on the western side of the school.

Our first submission was made to Rotherham Borough Council for approval.

Month after month, meeting after frustrating meeting had taken place involving Newman School, Rotherham Council, Fortem and Eurovia representatives. With the prospect of more meetings to come, Tom and I were constantly striving to reach an agreement that satisfied the council's criteria.

I was often in despair and frustrated that we would never get this path started, let alone constructed. I remember telling John Ryan, school caretaker, who was involved during all the meetings as an influential member of the school team, 'This is so frustrating, we must keep going, it's about the kids.'

Eventually, and now well into 2017, we finally received permission to construct the path after Tom, who had remained patient throughout, carefully steered our project through all the obstacles presented.

It was agreed that work would begin during the 2017

summer school holidays, which worked well within the four-week estimated construction programme.

Orders had also been placed to provide the playground equipment for the lower playground. Work would start and be installed at the same time as the path construction and be ready for the children after their summer break.

The large earth moving plant and equipment arrived at the start of the summer holidays and shortly after the grass-cutting ceremony had taken place, work on the path got underway.

It was such a thrilling sight to see the start of the final piece of the challenge clicking into place and at last getting underway, as the plant and bulldozer moved into position ready to start.

I could see right from the start that, as the dense undergrowth was cleared and the profile of the meandering path had been clearly cut through the woods, that the route we had planned was spot on. It looked just magical!

Enthusiastically, Tom and the volunteers from Sitwell Rotary, who had set up a labour force rota, worked together with the young Fortem project management team and Eurovia plant drivers. In total our labour force of over sixty people during the four-week construction made excellent progress to the sub-ground works of the path.

The large tarmac laying plant finally moved in, followed by a stream of lorries carrying the hot tarmac, and provided the amazing transformation. This topped off the huge amount of backbreaking groundwork that had taken place over the past three and a half weeks.

The Path to Success

This path was now beginning to look like a mini-miracle. A special mini-miracle, in fact probably the best mini-miracle ever. Sorry, getting a bit carried away, but I am sure you understand what this path meant to me and would mean to the pupils of Newman School.

During the final couple of days, a plethora of Sitwell Rotarians moved on site to re-seed damaged areas, level off soil heaps, secure multi-coloured benches and erect safety barriers down the slope at the far end of the path. In all they selflessly completed the 101 little jobs that would enhance the final appearance of this amazing path.

Howard Hughes, another Sitwell Rotarian, had designed and fabricated a high-quality gate that linked across and cordoned off the school driveway to the entrance of the newly formed path, making it safe from constant school traffic.

All this finishing work was carried out after the path had been completed, in order to have it ready for the children's return and the opening ceremony had been planned for Tuesday 12th September 2017.

A beautiful new four-seater teak bench had been donated to the school by Zoe Willoughby in remembrance of her father Peter, who had sadly recently passed away. The bench had arrived earlier in the week, together with the polished brass remembrance plaque.

We had agreed that the bench would provide a great addition to the project and would give the children an opportunity to have a rest at a quiet area on the path in comfort.

I first met Zoe during the sixty-fourth marathon which was sponsored by her local running club, Valley Hill Runners. There was a dozen or so club members who accompanied me after a Saturday morning park run from Concord Park.

Zoe had managed, for the first time ever, to run a marathon. We became good friends after sharing a day of camaraderie created by the run and during adverse weather conditions.

The sturdy bench was, after John Ryan had earlier given it a good coating of varnish, transported to its final location at the bottom corner of the path, where I was able to bolt the legs into the tarmac for safety.

We were now onto the final touches as John and I managed to erect and bolt down the commemorative plaque, on the bottom edge of the lower playground.

Disappointingly, however, the wheelchair roundabout would be out of bounds for a few days, due to a slight fabrication problem with one of the parts.

The long-awaited day finally arrived and, as Maureen and I arrived at the school, we were surprised to see just how many people had gathered to witness the final stage of my challenge.

Paul Sylvester, the newly appointed head of the school, greeted us outside reception and, after a minute of pleasantries with selected guests, we walked to the far end of the school. This area had been cordoned off with coloured buntings and set up with a number of chairs for the mayor and selected guests for the ribbon cutting.

I was pleased to see that the media was well represented. BBC, ITV and Sheffield Live TV, together with Radio Sheffield and news photographers, were all set up in strategic positions in the upper playground.

Paul opened the proceedings, making a heart-warming speech about what the path would mean for the children of Newman School, thanking everyone for their hard work and help during the construction of the amazing path, before handing over to me.

A slight panic ensued as I had searched for the speech that I had spent hours on the previous evening. I couldn't find it anywhere! Ah well, I was just going to have to talk from the heart and deliver an impromptu account of what the moment meant to me.

I went on to describe exactly what the path had meant to me from its original conception, now more than a couple of years ago, to that very special day.

I do believe, by the time I had finished talking, and had invited Eve with scissors in hand to join me, that everyone understood exactly why I challenged myself to run over 2,100 miles.

At around 11:30am, on Tuesday 12th November 2017, I invited our mayor, Cllr Eve Rose Keenan, to cut the ribbon and declare the path *open*! My chest was heaving with pride and satisfaction by that stage; I was on cloud nine, and once again just managing to suppress my emotional feelings.

Eve cut the ribbon and turned to me with a huge grin on her face as the crowd stepped forward on to the path for the first time. They were preceded by enthusiastic children in their wheelchairs who were being held back from racing off in excitement by some of the teachers. What an unforgettable sight. It will remain with me forever!

We came to a stop at the bench in the corner of the first section of the path where Zoe, her mother Susan Tanner and our mayor were sat being photographed. They were surrounded by a large group of supporters and children, while an interview, conducted by Andy Kershaw, went out live on Radio Sheffield. Rony was in the studio, rounding off the support they had given me during my challenge over the weeks and beyond.

The inaugural walk around the field concluded at the lower playground, after meandering through the woods that had seen the transformation over the holidays.

Work installing the specialist playground equipment had been also completed, other than the wheelchair roundabout, which unfortunately was still cordoned off.

Everyone was patiently waiting for me to arrive in order to complete the ceremony and bring this incredible event to a conclusion. BBC and ITV reporters were set up with cameras at the ready.

There was one more important function yet to be carried out before I was ready to call it a day: unveiling the commemorative plaque that I had lovingly managed to fabricate some weeks ago.

With the help of my good friend John Ryan, the stand, specially made so that the plaque was visible to wheelchair users, had been bolted down on a plinth of concrete.

Once again Eve Rose, who had been invited to perform the unveiling, stepped forward to say little more than, 'It gives me great pleasure to unveil this plaque,' followed by a huge cheer from everyone as she removed the cover that had been draped over the fourteen-inch-by-twelve-inch commemorative plaque.

Time for interviews, giving me the opportunity once again to talk about the amazing school that had played a huge part in mine and Maureen's lives over the past two and a half years.

I was more than happy to go along with the media. After

all, they had played a significant part in my journey during this challenge.

The day finally came to an end after countless thanks and heartfelt comments from friends, teachers and appreciative staff, who would undoubtedly make full use of these new additions to the school.

After a well-deserved cuppa with headteacher Paul, Maureen and I breathed a huge sigh of relief and headed for home.

Who says dreams don't come true?

*

Guest Contribution

John Ryan, caretaker at Newman School

I first became aware of John Ryan when I visited the school during the trike handover and realised that he was much, much more than just a caretaker. John holds Newman School and its children close to his heart, tirelessly going out of his way day in, day out to provide as good an environment as is possible. We became and will remain good friends.

Ray Matthews

When I first heard of the name Ray Matthews and learned of his intentions to raise money for the children of our school, I greeted it with a sense of bewilderment and disbelief.

Here was this man who wanted to run seventy-five

marathons in seventy-five days for his seventy-fifth birthday. I mean, who in their right mind would think they could even attempt to do that at any age, let alone at seventy-five! Then I met Ray.

His motives were truly awe-inspiring, not only for his fundraising intentions but because he wanted to make a difference to our children's physical, social, emotional and mental health; he wanted to do something that would improve their quality of life.

We are a special needs school and our children, who range from aged two to nineteen, have mild to chronic physical and learning disabilities and, for some, short life expectancy. However, despite the challenges that confront these children, it is a happy environment that holds its pupils dear to its heart. Unfortunately, our building is a victim of its age, its history and its grade II status. It is, however, in a beautiful setting with woods and trees all around and a very large, beautiful field to its front.

Despite its wonderful setting, our playing field was mostly inaccessible to pupils who use wheelchairs; they simply could not access the field unless we had long spells of dry weather that would bake the ground and stop the chairs from getting stuck.

Thus, Ray came up with the idea of constructing an accessible tarmac path around the edge of the field and through two small woodland areas.

It was never going to be a straightforward process and Ray has been unbowed and resolute when he has had to battle seemingly needless bureaucracy! His determination is admirable and he would often say to me, 'It's about the kids, John.'

Please do not let the installation of this path seem trivial. It was far from it. Ray knew that exercise, fresh air and nature would have a positive impact for our school.

Day in, day out that path is used with immense benefit, enabling children in wheelchairs to join their friends and gain greater independence. They can enjoy parts of the grounds that they couldn't before and they can even go in the woods. Outstanding!

It is not only the children in wheelchairs who profit from this. Those pupils who prefer their own company now have a place they can find peace, quiet and solitude.

We have benches along the path where friends can sit and enjoy a conversation and a school therapy dog that pupils (including those in chairs) can take for a walk. The relaxed nature of this wooded environment also offers a place that staff and pupils can use for sensitive discussions, for counselling, reassurance talks and confidence-building. It is a true aid to all aspects of positive mental health.

The path has become a place of joy and laughter!

It can never be underestimated how much this simple project has benefited us. Each and every class enjoys and reaps the rewards from this long stretch of tarmac. It is *all* down to Ray Matthews!

On a personal level, he is equally incredible and I count myself lucky not only to have met him but to call him a friend. His enthusiasm is infectious and his determination is phenomenal. Moreover, he is just a bloomin' nice, down-to-earth bloke.

As if his contribution to the path wasn't enough, he has maintained links with the school and supports us in many other ways. He joins us for other fundraising events and attends assemblies and award ceremonies. He has given inspirational talks and is always just a phone call away. Newman School is truly indebted to him.

Even recently, during the pandemic when the Rotherham 10K had to be cancelled, he asked people to do the distances individually to raise funds for Age UK Rotherham. I phoned Ray to say I would run the usual 10K course but that I would run it with the school's therapy dog to encourage further donations.

On the day, there was Ray on his bike, with a press photographer in tow, providing encouragement all the way round.

I have nothing but praise and admiration for Ray. His legacy will be timeless. He inspires people who then go on and add value to their communities. That in itself is a great skill of a fabulous character.

Ray is wonderfully selfless and such is his level of humanity that he applies his whole being to improve the lives of those less fortunate than most.

Quite simply, Ray is one of Rotherham's finest and deserves the admiration of all.

14

London calling

The experiences I had in 2016 were always going to be hard to beat, but those years that followed turned out to be just as amazing. It was hard to keep up with the events that were unfolding in rapid succession, both in my hometown in Rotherham and further afield in the bright lights of London.

The step into completely new territories started when I received the first of many official invitations to a glittering award ceremony – the British Citizens Award at the Palace of Westminster hosted by Bradley Walsh. What an incredible honour to be receiving such a prestigious award in recognition of fundraising and services to our community. The award would take place in January 2017, hosted by the Rt Hon Lord Dholakia.

My invited guests for the evening part of the ceremony were Adam and Charlotte, who had booked a hotel just around the corner from Maureen and me, close to King's Cross Station.

'Let's make a weekend of it,' I had suggested, and made a booking for us to see *Kinky Boots* the musical on the Friday evening. I was so looking forward to the show, having heard nothing but great reviews.

More interestingly, the very talented Dom Tribuzio, son of Marina Tune, a good friend of mine, was the musical's dance captain and would also be playing the policeman.

I contacted Dom, through Marina, and made plans to meet up after the show in the Retro Bar, a small pub in the West End that the performing cast frequent, just around the corner from the Adelphi Theatre.

The *Kinky Boots* show lived up to all expectations. A wonderful show, made even better by the seating upgrade which came as a pleasant surprise to us as we arrived to collect our tickets in the foyer. Not sure, but I suspect that Dom had something to do with this expensive upgrade.

We were ushered to front seats on the central first floor, which gave us unrestricted viewing of the entire stage.

The evening was rounded off in style. After a great show, we finally got to meet the very charismatic Dom at the Retro Bar over a glass of lager (they don't serve pints at the 'Break a Leg' bar).

I passed on his mum's good wishes and spent an informative half hour learning about the show's choreography, in which Dom had had a huge part to play. With a promise to provide a full cast signed copy of tonight's programme for Charlotte, we said our goodbyes. The fully signed programme arrived a couple of weeks later.

During the afternoon of the awards each of the recipients, twenty-nine of us, I believe, received their prestigious medals from Bradley Walsh and sponsors. Maureen and I met some amazing recipients of various British Citizen Awards. We mingled with them for an hour or so whilst we tucked into our table of nibbles (sandwiches with all the crusts cut off) before heading outside to meet Adam and Charlotte.

A tour of the city was planned in an open-top red bus which, decorated with large banners, displayed the identities of the privileged passengers. The bus was waiting opposite the Palace of Westminster, close to the grassy park area where so many TV interviews take place.

Shortly after organised group photos were taken, our entire party was invited to take part in the continued celebrations. We proudly toured around the city, waving to the onlooking crowd below like we were royalty!

It was at the start of the evening celebrations, as we all congregated in a large domed room inside the Palace of Westminster, where I first became aware of our opening keynote speaker, Lonnie Mayne.

Lonnie was dressed in a smart mid-blue business suit but most unusually was sporting a pair of bright red sneakers with white coloured laces. He walked confidently onto the stage. 'Who is this guy?' I wondered.

I was mesmerised listening to the American deliver a very powerful positive speech about how influential his professional wrestler father had been in his life. As a young boy, he had watched his father perform at the famous Carnegie Hall. His father wore bright red boxing boots in the ring; the effect that had on him cleverly set the theme for his talk.

He went on to describe how using the Red Shoes Living image had become a way of life that he promotes.

The red shoes certainly stand out and, through his speech, the shoes represented and created a symbol of awareness of humanity and how through respect and kindness a better working environment can be achieved.

Quite clearly, people matter to him.

This twenty-minute speech had me on the edge of my seat and became the catalyst for future plans that were beginning to form in my head.

I was well and truly hooked. 'I want to become a motivational speaker,' I thought. I couldn't wait to put plans for raising more funds for Newman School into practice.

Bradley Walsh took over for the evening and, after a short introduction, invited each recipient in turn onto the stage to collect their certificates to add to the medal.

I was miles away in thought, planning my new role as a speaker, when I suddenly realised that my name and running profile photo had appeared on the large screen above the stage.

'Come on, Ray,' Bradley shouted, as I stood up to make that long walk from my seat to the stage. 'I have been trying to interview Ray for ages,' he said, 'but I've not been able to catch him.' That certainly put me at ease as the audience burst into laughter.

I had been asked just prior to the awards if I wanted to give a short speech during my presentation, as time was limited and only a few recipients were being allowed that privilege.

'You bet I do!' was my answer. I wanted to tell everyone about Newman School and the angels who provide these children with the happiest of environments possible.

And you bet I did, because shortly after the introduction and certificate presentation, Bradley handed me the microphone and stepped back a few paces.

This was my golden opportunity. I was determined that everyone in the hall would know about Newman School and why I had taken on that seventy-five-marathon challenge. I put my heart and soul into the impromptu speech, conscious now that my mind was made up, that this was to be the first of many talks that would follow.

After my speech to the very attentive and silent audience ended, and whilst a heart-warming round of applause was being delivered, I turned to Bradley Walsh to hand back the microphone. He took the microphone from me and, as he wiped away a tear or two, he shook my hand warmly and simply said, 'Thank you, Ray.' The sincerity of that simple comment made me realise just what a powerful effect that well-spoken, sincere, passionate words can have.

The evening came to an end after the mandatory TV and press interviews had taken place, each one wanting further information about my challenge and the school I had talked about during my speech.

Shortly after the interviews, I met Lonnie and, during our conversation, I mentioned the word 'passion'. A word, well, much more than just a word, more of a statement, really, that stood out and meant so much to both of us. A word that we would both frequently use in the future.

Passion.

*

Once my feet were finally back on the ground in Rotherham, it wasn't long before news of the next accolade was announced.

I'd been invited to become a patron of Newman School, an honour I could hardly refuse. But just over a month after the path-opening ceremony was completed, I was contacted by one of the ITV producers with a request to meet Adam Fowler at Newman School.

It was a little bit vague really, but he did mention something along the lines of doing some filming about the school.

I arrived at the school and, after signing in, met up with the headteacher, Paul, who seemed similarly elusive about what was happening. I should have guessed that there was more to this meeting as we walked down to the path in the woods and met Adam and his cameraman.

We set up shop, as it were, on the path in the woods, joined by Rich Sales, the school's very talented photographer. After greetings, I was directed into position ready to be interviewed, wondering what I was about to be asked.

Having completed the camera and sound checks and ensuring that I was stood in the right light, Adam, looking directly into the camera, introduced me and my achievements over the past year.

He slowly turned to me and said, 'Ray, I have to tell you that you have been nominated for the ITV Pride of Britain Award. How does that make you feel?'

I was gobsmacked. 'Wow!' I declared. 'That's incredible, what an honour to be nominated for such an amazing award!'

Adam looked at me with a smile on his face, bent down and fumbled inside a briefcase that was on the ground just to one side of him. He stood up and, turning to me, said, 'Well, my friend, I have to tell you that...' and after a slight pause for effect, continued, 'Ray, you have actually been awarded the Pride of Britain Award!'

He then handed me the colourful trophy that he had concealed behind his back. 'How do you feel now?' he said.

Hell's bells! I was speechless, and just stood there looking at *my* trophy.

Having watched the award ceremony year after year, I

knew that there are some amazing people out there doing extraordinary things for charity. Now I, Ray Matthews, had only gone and won that year's much-coveted award.

'What a humbling experience Adam,' I said, once I was confident my voice wouldn't break down with emotion. 'I am so proud and honoured. This award will be dedicated to all the amazing people who have helped me to succeed during my challenge.'

I should have known there was something afoot, as I had received a vague email that morning from a charity organisation in Doncaster, just congratulating me on my award without any explanation. I had thought, 'What award? Must be a scam,' and deleted the message without giving it another thought.

To clarify, my award represents the Pride of Britain, Yorkshire area. The recipient, along with the rest of the area winners, are automatically entered into the national final, held in London later in the year.

After the marathon challenge had ended, Maureen and I had agreed that we should spend more time together and travel the world. This was why, on the evening of the national awards, we were on the other side of the world in Alice Springs, Australia. Disappointed that we were to miss this amazing ceremony, we were proud that our son, Gary, and beautiful granddaughter, Holly, were able to represent us.

The national Pride of Britain Award ceremony, hosted by Carol Vorderman, is by far the largest viewed televised event of its kind.

During the evening Holly mingled comfortably with an array of invited celebrities, giving her the opportunity to feel like one of the celebrities herself, she later told me.

They had the time of their lives at the awards, especially Holly, who had been in huge demand, looking more like a celebrity herself. She was bubbling with excitement during our Skype call a few hours later, as she relayed the details of the evening, telling me how proud she was of her grandad. Aah…

How amazing is technology when we were able to talk to one another, just under ten thousand miles away, as though we were in the same room together? Fantastic.

Unfortunately, I didn't win the prestigious national award. I can't say I wasn't disappointed as it would have been great to have brought the trophy back to Yorkshire. Rest assured, the young boy who did thoroughly deserved this prestigious title.

*

Back on home turf and my diary was once again filling up with events, particularly in Rotherham. A get-together with Sean took place shortly after the 'I want to become a motivational speaker' thoughts at the British Citizens Awards. We discussed my new proposed speaking role and how we could raise more cash for the fundraising pot.

Sean suggested an 'Evening with Ray' at the Crown Hotel in Bawtry: a black-tie dinner that we could turn into a fundraising event.

Sounded like a fantastic idea to me, then suddenly the best idea ever entered my mind.

'What about inviting Michael Parkinson to host the evening and interview me?' I said to a bewildered-looking Sean.

'Don't give much hope to that happening, Ray,' he said, shaking his head. 'He's been retired some time now.'

I knew he was from Cudworth in Barnsley, not all that far away, I thought. 'Can you get me his phone number, Sean, and I will ask the question.' If you don't ask you don't get has always been my philosophy.

I made the call less than a week later but unfortunately Michael was out of the country visiting relations in Australia and wouldn't be back in time.

What a coup that would have been if I could have pulled it off.

Sam Cooper, deputy news editor of the Rotherham Advertiser at that time, more than ably filled the bill, with the assistance from Dave Poucher. Dave organised and provided the rolling collage of action photos, displayed onto the large screen behind us throughout the evening's questions and answers.

Sam asked all the right questions. Of course, he was more than familiar with my life story, having reported on my many activities and challenges over the years. This gave me the opportunity to deliver relevant and interesting stories in a completely relaxed manner. A thoroughly enjoyable evening that culminated in a standing ovation which lasted an embarrassingly long time.

The evening turned out to be a huge success, made possible by the large number of friends, colleagues and running mates in attendance. All these worthy citizens had very generously contributed to the auction and table booking fee. One of my paintings even returned a record auction fee by phone bid! Don't you just love it when your plans become a success?

*

Soon enough it was time to put my new-found love of public speaking to the test once again.

The incoming mayor of Rotherham, Cllr Eve Rose Keenan, had requested I provide an after-dinner speech at her inauguration.

Becoming the Rotherham mayor, a historic ceremony that dates back to 1824, is a pretty lengthy affair that takes up most of the day. After the inauguration in the council chambers, it comprises a procession, surrounded by influential dignitaries, around the town centre and back to Rotherham Town Hall for celebrations, after a short service in the All Saints' Minster.

Maureen and I had been invited, along with a select number of friends of Eve and her husband Pat, to the evening meal where, towards the end of the evening, I was introduced and invited to deliver my speech – prepared this time…

Don't you just love the feeling when you realise you're in control? The guests were under my spell as I spoke for around twenty minutes about our new mayor, how we first met in running gear at the stadium and how our friendship had blossomed. I really didn't want the speech to end. Just magic!

*

What an interesting and diverse life I was now leading, as I was being invited to speak at many functions, conferences and award ceremonies.

It was during the Rotherham Community award ceremony, at the Carlton Park Hotel in Rotherham, where Maureen and I met the Deputy Lieutenant of South Yorkshire, Bob Dyson, for the first of many events.

An array of influential guests sat at our table waiting for the awards to get underway. As Maureen and I took our seats, we were introduced to Janet Wheatley MBE, CEO of Voluntary Action Rotherham, who then went on to introduce her invited distinguished guests. These included the High Sheriff of Yorkshire, Steven Ingrams, and our new mayor Eve Rose and her husband Pat. Name-dropper!

I was particularly pleased to witness, among the award winners, young Vicky Bezza, a partially sighted former Newman School pupil. Vicky was presented with one of the awards for her amazing work in the community. She also managed a radio show every Friday afternoon. Amazing, well done, Vicky.

As the event seemed to be coming to a conclusion, an announcement inviting Eve to the stage was made to bring the event to a close, or so I thought.

No sooner had she picked up the microphone than the large screen behind her burst into life with a film about me.

Now it all made sense and answered a question that had been niggling me for a few weeks. What had happened to the promotional Rotherham film that I had participated in a couple of months ago?

I had been contacted a few months earlier by a private film company who had been hired by Voluntary Action Rotherham to put together a promotional film highlighting what's good about our town and its people. I had been completely suckered in with this one as, using a drone, they had filmed me running across fields and woodland around Maltby.

Once again, Eve delivered a very touching speech about my recent fundraising work in and around Rotherham, highlighting the work in which I was now involved, championing "Run a Mile a Day with Ray".

This was an initiative for Rotherham schools to combat obesity in children. Eve had also taken part by running a mile with me and some of the children.

'It gives me immense pleasure to announce that the Special Recognition Award for Rotherham Community Achievement goes to my great friend, Ray Matthews,' she suddenly announced, inviting me onto the stage to collect the trophy.

I was a becoming a dab hand at delivering impromptu speeches nowadays and managed a shortened version of a great, much longer acceptance speech to bring the event to a close.

*

Don't worry, my friend, we're coming towards the end of all the accolades and great surprises. But there is just one more surprise that would be sacrilege not to mention.

It all started when a very official-looking envelope dropped through our letterbox.

'Maureen,' I shouted as I picked up the distinctive cream-coloured envelope with the heavily embossed Royal Coat of Arms emblem in the left corner. 'It looks as though the Queen's sent us a letter,' I said as I walked into the room with a huge grin on my face, carefully opening the envelope.

> *The Lord Chamberlain is commanded by Her Majesty to invite Mr and Mrs Raymond Matthews to a garden party at Buckingham Palace.*

'Now this is something rather special,' I thought, and of course we accepted the invitation, be rather rude not to.

Another extended trip to the capital which provided the opportunity to take in a couple of shows. We would also be able to do the touristy bits that we never seemed to have time for when taking part in the many London marathons over the past few years.

Our first show was *Wicked* at the Apollo Victoria theatre for the Monday evening before the Tuesday garden party. As a further treat, I booked for us to see the Wednesday-evening performance of *The Lion King* at the Lyceum Theatre.

Just after midday, on Tuesday 21st May 2019, we shared a taxi from King's Cross Station with another couple who were, like Maureen and me, dressed to impress in our Sunday best.

Our taxi, which seemed to take forever, drove right up to the main gates of Buckingham Palace, having driven down Constitution Hill, through the restricted closed section at the Palace end.

We alighted the taxi and took our time looking around at the very imposing bronze Victoria Memorial and the palace frontage that I had run past on many occasions. This time the area was free of coloured advertising buntings.

We made our entrance through the ornate wrought-iron gates, passing security into the grand red gravel palace forecourt.

It was time for photos and, let's be honest, we were without any doubt soaking up the regal atmosphere as more and more guests arrived. You don't get these opportunities every day, I was thinking. Then, when I was just about to take the final photo of Maureen, one of the photogenic guards, in full military uniform, stepped alongside her to make for a special photograph with the palace in the background.

Following the crowds, who all seemed to know where to

go, we entered a long narrow palatial passage that ran the entire width of the palace. This room, decorated with period paintings, ornate furniture and well-trodden red carpet that showed signs of a bygone era, opened out at the far end into the afternoon sun.

The rear of the palace, a view that we the public never normally get to see, opened up below us as we stood at the top of around twenty steps that led down to a well-manicured grassed area the size of a large cricket ground.

We could see a rather posh marquee, which was already filling up with dignitaries and overseas guests, some 250 yards away.

We settled into what we assumed would be a strategic spot alongside other guests, close to the path that we anticipated the Queen and her entourage would be using.

Having managed to secure a seat for Maureen and, whilst being entertained by a number of military bands, I headed across the lawn to a low-level tent area to take advantage of the snacks and beverages. As usual, I was starving.

Ever wondered how many small Buckingham Palace crested plates end up in handbags or pockets as souvenirs? Before you ask, no, we didn't!

Excitement among the crowd was the giveaway that the Royal Party was making an entrance, as everyone stood trying to get the best view.

Patience prevailed as we were soon able to clearly see Prince William and Kate as they strolled down the avenue of guests followed by the Queen, surrounded by her top hat and tailed entourage.

I remember taking a 360-degree look around whilst we

waited for Her Majesty to return from the marquee, confirming the large security presence I would have expected with such a large attendance. I could see earpieces in formal-suited close attendants who were continually talking into closed fists. Whilst squinting in the afternoon sunlight, I could make out what looked like military snipers, strategically placed behind parapet stonework along the palace roof, alert and ready.

Even though I must have looked like James Bond in my best whistle and flute, I don't think she noticed me as Her Majesty, returning from the marquee, walked close by, still smiling and interacting with the crowd. She had the ability to make you feel special without uttering a word.

A very special afternoon at Buckingham Palace ended with a leisurely walk around the large lake admiring the gardens on the far side of the grounds, eventually leaving for the Victoria tube station by the Grosvenor Palace Road exit.

We enjoyed a quiet intimate evening meal at an Italian restaurant, close to King's Cross Station, before returning to our hotel to end our very special day.

Our final day in the capital was spent enjoying a pleasant afternoon doing the touristy bit, using our bus passes on the big red double-decker bus, departing from close to our hotel and heading to Trafalgar Square.

An hour, nowhere near enough time, was spent in the National Gallery admiring a few selected paintings before heading to Covent Garden for a spot of lunch and enjoying the street entertainment before making our way to the Lyceum Theatre.

The Lion King is a fantastic show, thoroughly entertaining and one of the best musicals we have seen during our trips to

London. We even used our bus passes to travel back to our hotel after the show around 11pm.

Perhaps this could be a good place to end our story. *But…*

*

Even though there have been many other amazing events worth recalling around this incredible time, I feel that my eightieth-birthday challenge is probably equally, if not more, rewarding than any.

My aim, as a birthday present once again, was, this time to raise much-needed funds for Age UK Rotherham. Like all charities, they had struggled during the pandemic to maintain the amazing services they provide for our ageing population.

My latest challenge was to invite at least eighty schools from around South Yorkshire to raise at least £80 by running a minimum of eighty miles. I had spent over three weeks successfully visiting many schools, talking about the virtues of running a mile a day and encouraging the schools to sign up to the 80-80-80 challenge.

Having randomly selected two schools to visit, on the morning of my eightieth birthday I met with ITV and was followed into Wickersley Northfield Primary School. Waiting there was a class of excited children ready to run the mile with me down on one of their playgrounds. Even the ITV reporter managed to run a few laps with the children and me!

Shortly after lunch, I was reacquainted with Nicola from Look North as the BBC filmed the children and me at my former school, St Bede's Catholic Primary School. Not only did they run the mile, but they also surprised me with a birthday cake and presented me with a Japanese miniature maple tree which has since been planted in our garden.

What an amazing day, firstly receiving in excess of five hundred handmade birthday cards, and secondly we estimated that around twenty-five thousand schoolchildren from across South Yorkshire 'Ran a Mile with Ray' on my birthday. I don't think I could better that amazing feeling.

The last word, surely, belongs to the children!

Epilogue

Life has been incredibly exciting, providing amazing memories over the years. From an early age, meeting dedicated people who not only taught me how to box but provided the knowledge and instilled in me a way of life that has been the backbone of my existence.

'It's a gift. Only special young boys have ginger hair,' Mum told me during a sensitive discussion. In spite of the gift, and because of my rebellious nature, I felt different to every other pupil at St Bede's School because of my ginger hair.

I really did resent the mockery and bullying that came from older classmates because of my almost red hair. Looking back, how ironic is it that the very thing that plagued my life then led me to becoming what I am today by the choices I made at such an early age?

Since those early formative years, I have continued to take on the seemingly impossible (other people's comments) self-inflicted challenges and enthusiastically made them possible through belief, providing a real sense of achievement year after year.

Be true to yourself. Be content in the knowledge that you have done your best to become the very best that's possible.

Don't wait for opportunities; they never happen. Create your own and be willing to stand on that start line, because vision without action is nothing more than a dream. Investing in yourself will not only improve your life; it will also improve the lives of those around you.

So, what's next? What is the future? A question asked more than ever of late. As I age, it's becoming increasingly more important to remain fit and healthy as I continue to invest more time in schools teaching, by example, the virtues of health and wellbeing to our children which is freely available through exercise.

'Movement is medicine'. A statement that not only applies to children but also to our ageing population. Getting that message across in a way that inspires and passionately fuses the mind to achieve more is my main aim, using a set of rules that have worked well over the years.

1. Trust in yourself. Don't waste your time living your life to other people's expectations.
2. Don't be afraid to fail. You're already a winner when you stand on the start line.
3. Ignore the doubters; they will never understand. Rely on Rule 1.
4. Work like hell to succeed.
5. Don't forget to give something back.

*

In conclusion, only those who would risk going too far can possibly find out how far you can go. With that in mind, I would like to invite you all to cheer me over the finish line when I fulfil my promise of running a hundred marathons in a hundred days starting on my hundredth birthday, and finishing on Tuesday 8th October 2041. Only wimps with a valid letter from their mum will be excused.

Acknowledgements

I would like to express my profound thanks to my friends Amber and Chris for their help, patience and advice during the long months of bringing this book to a successful conclusion. Thank you.